The Castles of Northumberland

Premium Edition

Stephen Wood

Orwell House

First Edition published 2023 by Orwell House Publishing

This Premium Edition published 2023 by Orwell House Publishing

ISBN 978 1 8384688 5 9

Set in Garamond 11 pt

This book is dedicated to the Duke of Normandy, otherwise known as
William the Conqueror, King William 1st of England
and William the Bastard

to whom we owe the heritage of our great castles, and without whose
1066 invasion we would all be a little bit less French

INDEX

1. Alnwick
2. Aydon
3. Bamburgh
4. Barmoor
5. Beaufront
6. Belford
7. Bellister
8. Belsay
9. Berwick
10. Blenkinsopp
11. Bothal
12. Bywell
13. Cartington
14. Chillingham
15. Chipchase
16. Dilston
17. Dunstanburgh
18. Edlingham
19. Elsdon
20. Etal
21. Featherstone
22. Ford
23. Halton
24. Harbottle
25. Haughton
26. Langley
27. Lindisfarne
28. Mitford
29. Morpeth
30. Newcastle
31. Norham
32. Prudhoe
33. Thirlwall
34. Twizell
35. Tynemouth
36. Warkworth
Ordnance Survey OpenSourceData
Site locations are approximate
Grantshouse
Eyemouth
Duns
Berwick-upon-Tweed
Greenlaw
Norham
R Tweed
Holy Island
Coldstream
Etal
Northumberland Coast
Kelso
Belford
Seahouses
Wooler
Jedburgh
The Cheviot Hills
Longhoughton
Alnwick
Edlingham
Alnmouth
Amble
NORTHUMBERLAND
Rothbury
Kielder
Otterburn
Ashington
Newbiggin-by-the-Sea
R North Tyne
Morpeth
Bedlington
Bellingham
Belsay
Blyth
Cramlington
Whitley Bay
NEWCASTLE UPON TYNE
Wallsend
Tynemouth
Haydon Bridge
Corbridge
South Shields
Haltwhistle
Jarrow
A1
A6105
A6112
A697
A698
A68
A69
A1068
A189
A193
A19
A6079

A WORD ABOUT WILLIAM

William the Conqueror, architect of England, single-handedly responsible for the aristocracy, landed estates, the nobility, Lords and Ladies and the Great Castles, was born in about 1028 in Normandy.

William was given the nickname "*the Bastard*" not because he was a particularly vindictive so-and-so, although he may have been that as well, but because he was the illegitimate son of Duke Robert I of Normandy and his mistress Herleve.

William the Conqueror
Official Portrait, 1080

Ordinarily, illegitimacy would have been a significant bar to his social and political status, and indeed to his succession, but William was fortunate and on his father's death in 1035 he was recognised by his family as the heir - an exception to the general rule, and a decision that had the most profound consequences for England, its people, and in due course its castles.

Normandy and William's family have a complicated history bound up with the Vikings and the Gallo-Frank inhabitants of the area we now know as northern France, and all that is far beyond the scope of this book. Suffice it to say that he was, obviously and from a modern perspective, French. From 1047 onwards and in the course of various campaigns, William gained enormous military experience and by the time of his invasion of England in 1066 he was a highly respected and ruthless military commander who inspired both fear and respect beyond his homeland.

William's claim to the English throne was based on his assertion that, in 1051, his distant cousin Edward the Confessor had promised him the throne and that Harold II - having sworn in 1064 to uphold William's right to succeed to that throne - was going back on the deal.

William took seven months to prepare his invasion force, using some 600 transport ships to carry around 7,000 men, including 2,000-3,000 cavalry, across the Channel. On 28 September 1066 he landed unopposed at Pevensey and, within a few days, raised fortifications at Hastings. At the time King Harold was Up North seeing off the Vikings under the King of Norway at the Battle of Stamford Bridge near York. Upon learning of William's invasion he undertook a forced march south which punished his already exhausted troops even more. Covering 250 miles in some nine days, by the time they got to Hastings they must have been, as we might say today, in need of a beer.

But there was no time for that, and the outcome is well-known. Although Harold had strength of numbers and geographical advantage William had archers and cavalry, both of which the English forces lacked. During a Norman assault, Harold was killed - hit by an arrow and then mown down by the sword of a mounted knight.

From the Bayeux Tapestry - Harold appears to be hit in the eye

Whether he was really hit in the eye as popular history tells us is something of debate, in spite of the depiction in the Bayeux tapestry. Anyway, one way or the other he was done for, the English forces fled and William stuck his flag in the soil of England.

William was crowned on Christmas Day 1066 in Westminster Abbey. However, it took him six years to complete his conquest, having to face constant plotting and fighting including raids and uprisings in the south of England, in the Welsh Marches, and in Devon and Cornwall. From his supporters William appointed earls who, in all parts of the kingdom, undertook to guard the threatened frontiers and maintain internal security in return for land.

In 1069 in the north of England William battled with the Danes who still refused to go away. He defeated them and then systematically devastated Mercia and Northumbria to deprive the Danes of their supplies and prevent recovery of English resistance. Churches and monasteries were burnt, and agricultural land was laid to waste, creating a famine for the unarmed and mostly peasant population which lasted at least nine years. William made it perfectly plain who was boss, and woe-betide anyone who thought otherwise.

Further north, where the boundary with Scotland was unclear, there was continued unrest, so William commenced a castle-building campaign to stamp his authority in those places it was needed. Originally these castles were motte and bailey constructions, wooden towers on earth mounds surrounded by earth ramparts, but stone fortifications soon followed. In accordance with his policy of showing precisely who was in charge William confiscated land from English nobles and by the end of his reign over 80 castles had been built throughout his kingdom – and so the new Norman feudal order began.

William created up to 180 honours - lands scattered throughout the Kingdom, with a castle as the governing centre. As a result he had some 5,000 knights at his disposal to repress rebellions and keep the riff-raff in order. The King's principal tenants - barons and favoured noblemen - in turn created knights and private armies centred around their private castles. Thus arose a system of local administration and enforcement. By the end of William's reign, a small group of the King's favoured nobility had acquired, by confiscation, theft and by the sword, about half of the land in England. A foreign aristocracy had been imposed as the new governing class of England.

The Domesday survey was prompted by the need to take stock of land holding in England, and to ensure the direct loyalty of William's feudal tenants. The survey resulted in the two-volume Domesday Book of 1086, which still exists today. The 1086 Oath of Salisbury was a gathering of William's 170 tenants-in-chief and other important landowners who took an oath of allegiance to the King.

The Tomb of William the Conqueror at Caen, Abbey of Saint-Étienne

William was buried in the abbey of St Stephen at Caen, the burial place of the first Norman king of England marked by a simple stone slab.

So, would our Great Castles have existed at all without William the Conqueror, King William I of England, William the Bastard? Possibly, even probably, but by no means for sure, and they would certainly not have evolved in the way that they did. For those whose interest, whose passion lies in those castles, William the Conqueror, bastard and King, is the man who gave us the heritage we value so highly today.

Warkworth Castle *Fred Vincent*

Cover photos of Alnwick Castle (front) and Warkworth Castle (back) by Ron Lyons

INTRODUCTION

Let's start with the Romans. With their centurions and legions they were the occupiers of our lands for the first 400 years of the first millennium, and there's no disputing that their legacy remains with us to this day. Don't ever ask "*What have the Romans ever done for us?*" without expecting a long, Monty Python list of the benefits they brought, and left us with. From 43 to 410 AD they imposed their laws, culture, military strength and governance on the people of Britain. They built forts, and of course in the north they built Hadrian's Wall – even then the Scots were a nuisance – but they did not build castles.

Then perhaps they got fed up with the English weather, or the food, or the relentless barbarian behaviour of the natives, or more likely the economics of maintaining a presence just didn't stack up, but for whatever reason the Romans upped and left in 410 AD. From then on for 6 centuries the Anglo-Saxon period took over, often known as the Dark Ages or the early medieval period, when proper castles weren't built either.

The Anglo-Saxon period came to an end in 1066 when our Patron, William the Conqueror, arrived with his Norman invaders and everything changed. As William established himself throughout the Anglo-Saxon lands he created baronies and distributed them to his noble friends and supporters. Those new Norman barons account for the proliferation of French-sounding names, like Yves de Vescy, Baron of Alnwick in 1096. As each baron sought to secure his new estates, fortifications arose – the beginnings of what we know today as the castles.

Artist's impression of a motte & bailey castle [Ipswich History]

In the far north defence and security were particularly important because of the proximity to the Scottish border. Every baron's lands were affected by the persistent conflicts in the borders, from full on battles to speculative, opportunistic raids by *Border Reivers*[14], raiders seeking to plunder livestock and whatever they could get their hands on. Thus, the barons either built, or adapted Anglo-Saxon defences, the motte and bailey – at first little more than an earth mound with a wooden stockade or enclosure and perhaps a ditch – and then before long the stone tower appeared, the keep with curtain walls, gatehouses, drawbridges and the features of the castle we think of today.

These days antagonism between the Scots and the English is mainly confined to the sports field or the political stage, but the occupiers of northern England had to contend with constant, armed and physical conflict. The strength of the castles built to protect the interests of the barons and landowners reflected that. Between the 12th and the 16th centuries a licence was required, from the King or from an authority such as a Bishop, to fortify a property with battlements and that sort of thing, a process known as *crenellation*[4]. Such was the need for defence that hundreds of such licences were issued.

And so over the years the strength and sophistication of castles evolved. They were strung out across the north providing family seats, comfortable and sometimes opulent living, and most importantly security.

Tower crenelations

Eventually however, the divided monarchies of England and Scotland came to an end when the English monarch Elizabeth I died without leaving an heir, and in 1603 the crown passed to her cousin James VI of Scotland, who at one and same time became King James I of England and thus by this *Union of Crowns*[5] England and Scotland were brought together under a single monarch. Of course, there's much more to it than a summary as simple as that, but although the unification didn't bring total peace in the borders, it did suppress much of the conflict and the need for highly strengthened castellate fortifications reduced. As a result many castles were then neglected and fell into disrepair and ruin.

As the centuries rolled by, the barons and nobility, earls and dukes, knights and lords had to contend with more than just the Scots. As the political landscape changed they had to choose their allegiances wisely. During the *Wars of the Roses*[3], 1455 – 1487, when the claim to the throne was contested between the Yorkists and the Lancastrians, and *The English Civil Wars*[2], 1642 – 1652, when the Royalists and Parliamentarians under Oliver Cromwell fought for the rule of England, those who chose to support the wrong side often lost their heads, or at least their castles and estates which were confiscated and given to those more supporting of whichever side was on the rise. Throughout the centuries many castles changed hands and families and dynasties came and went as a consequence of an unwise choice of allegiance.

So, some castles survived, and some didn't. Of those that did, some, like Bamburgh and Alnwick, have retained their status as great family seats. Some, like Langley, have turned into prestigious hotels, or wedding venues with prosecco and white marquees. Of those that have not, some have been preserved and curated by worthy institutions like English Heritage, presented as museums to the viewing public. Some have been dug up and subjected to intense archaeological research. And some have simply decayed away into crumbling stone, plundered of what could be salvaged.

The splendour of Northumbrian castles captured here with Lindisfarne in the foreground and the mighty Bamburgh castle rising in the distance - photo Paul Turner

There are more than 70 castle sites that survive throughout the modern-day county of Northumberland, and a lot more than that if you include the pele towers[6], watchtowers, bastles (a sort of fortified farm building) and that sort of thing. Some, like those at Bamburgh and Alnwick, are very well known. Others, less familiar, may be welcome new discoveries. That there are so many castles, or the remains of them, in Northumberland – more than in any other county in the country - is testament to the tumultuous years when the ancient kingdom of Northumbria, which stretched from Edinburgh to the Humber, witnessed centuries of warfare, raiding and constant conflict between England and Scotland. Each of these places, without exception and whatever their present condition, has a deep and fascinating history, and a book of this sort cannot begin to explore their detailed origins and how they have evolved through time. Most have been the subject of extensive, published archaeological and historical research, and for those inclined to learn more and delve deeper into their intriguing histories I have included some suggestions as to where further reading may be found.

The purpose of this book is to offer an introduction to these castles of Northumberland, and an idea of what the present-day visitor might expect. I have included, in so far as I have been able, details of a site's location, its ownership and stewardship, a brief history and details of its current status and on-site facilities. The photographs, I hope, will be helpful too, as well as attractive in themselves.

A "castle" is defined by the Oxford English Dictionary as "*a large building, typically of the medieval period, which is (or was formerly) fortified as a stronghold*". We tend to imagine a castle as built of heavy, substantial stone, castellated, with towers, pinnacles, arrow slits and turrets, but there is a wide variety of structures that might fall within the definition suggested by the OED, from simple watchtowers to fortified stately homes. For the purposes of this book I have stayed with the more common, popular idea of a castle, and with some exceptions where I have thought it appropriate, I have generally excluded sites which fall into the following categories:

- Manor houses, stately homes and properties the function of which was not principally, or at least significantly, defensive.
- Locations where the remaining structure has degraded to earthworks or only low protruding stonework.
- Pele towers, fortified keeps and watchtowers.
- Abbeys, churches, priories and places where the principal focus was religious

Nevertheless, there is a great diversity in the 36 sites I have chosen to include, from ruins where visitors are left to themselves to wander around amidst broken stonework, to places where exhibitions and entertainments are highly organized. They all have differing facilities, varying from the almost non-existent to the substantially commercial. In each case I have provided a brief overview of the facilities available, and to the best of my knowledge this is accurate at the time of publication. However, such things change from time to time, especially admission charges (if any) and access times. Visitors should check in advance for up-to-date details and usually the venue's website is as good as anywhere to obtain this information. Members of organisations such as English Heritage or The National Trust may receive free or discounted admission, and concessions are often available.

For many the history of these places is a fascinating thing, and to touch it, walk through it and tread in the footsteps of our ancestors is an exceptional and rewarding experience. The castles that arose in our lands over the centuries are a legacy that allows us a glimpse into that past, and none more so than the castles of Northumberland.

The castles are arranged throughout the book in alphabetical order.

ONE

ALNWICK CASTLE

It is not only the accident of alphabetical order that puts Alnwick Castle at the top of this list, but also that it is one of the largest, best restored, permanently inhabited castles in the country. Whether you have an appetite for history or an ambition to take a lesson in broomstick flying, Alnwick Castle is where all this, and more, is to be found. The very epitome of the English castle it has castellated curtain walls, pennants flying from high towers, and cannon adorning the battlements. Medieval architecture is combined with sumptuous staterooms, art and sculptures. There's a lot of history here, the legacy of bygone wars and the opulence of nobility.

Photo courtesy Alnwick Castle

For more than 7 centuries Alnwick Castle has been the ancestral home of the Percy family - the Earls, Dukes and Duchesses of Northumberland. The 1st Duchess, Elizabeth Percy (1716 – 1776) took on the restoration of the castle after it had fallen into disrepair, and she established it as the family's permanent home. On through the ages the title now rests with its present incumbent Ralph Percy, the 12th Duke of Northumberland who, with his wife Jane the Duchess, has developed and maintained the castle and its renowned gardens not only as their private residence but also as a major visitor and tourist attraction. It is the second largest inhabited castle in the country, next only to Windsor.

The origins of the castle lie, like so many, in the years following the Norman invasion of 1066. Such places, Alnwick included, were built to establish the status and power of the new Norman barons, in this case Yves de Vescy, Baron of Alnwick in 1096. At first a wood and earth motte and bailey construction, by the mid 12th century it had been rebuilt in stone. In 1309, Henry Percy, great-great grandfather of the celebrated Sir Henry (or Harry) Percy, nicknamed Hotspur for his audacious conduct in battle, purchased the site. In the following 40 years he and his son transformed this modest defence into a mighty border fortress. Towers and turrets were added around its curtain walls with a strong gatehouse at the entrance and a concealed postern gate[1] to the rear. The gateway to the keep was strengthened with the addition of two massive octagonal towers.

Over the following decades the castle underwent further strengthening and improvement, but in the late 17th century it fell into disrepair. The Percy family were not at that time permanently resident there and the misfortunes of war, especially raids by the Scots, the English Civil War[2] and the Wars of the Roses[3], had left it damaged and forlorn.

The castle painted by Canaletto about 1752

Aerial view by Fred Vincent

Restoration at the hands of the 1st Duchess was carried out in the 18th century, along with the layout of the grounds and gardens. The 19th century brought further improvements and the renovation of state apartments – grand, opulent rooms in the Italianate style. In the mid 20th century the castle was used as a teacher training college and student accommodation. A strong educational focus is maintained today.

When the branch line to Alnwick was constructed in 1850 it was perhaps, partly at least, the high status of the Percy family that resulted in the station buildings for this modest rural town being built in an especially grand style. Here were welcomed visiting VIPs, even royalty. Although that station no longer serves a railway, it is preserved as the home of Barter Books which claims to be the largest second-hand bookshop in the country. And it may well be. It's an Aladdin's cave of the written word. Its vast array of literature covers every possible genre from children's books to rare antiquities, while model trains chug around overhead at gallery level in acknowledgment of its railway heritage.

Cannon and heavy stone epitomise the strength of Alnwick Castle

Photos (left and below) Ron Lyons

The grand opulence of the castle's staterooms is beautifully presented here in the dining room (above), the library (left) and the upper chamber (below)

Photos courtesy of Alnwick Castle

Today, the castle is well-known for its association with the Harry Potter film franchise, as well as a location for other television and film productions, including Downton Abbey, Robin Hood: Prince of Thieves, Blackadder and many others. Children's activities, heavily influenced by the Harry Potter theme, are a major attraction with archery, hawking, swordsmanship and even broomstick flying among the varied entertainments available.

There are cafes and restaurant facilities, a gift shop, outdoor and indoor activities for both children and adults alike. There are indoor exhibitions and demonstration areas and from the battlements there are panoramic views. Permanent museum displays include the Regimental Museum of the Royal Northumberland Fusiliers. The world-renowned gardens include cascades, fountains and a huge treehouse complex.

Photos courtesy Alnwick Castle

There is much to be seen and visitors are free to explore the state-rooms and residence. Guided tours around the lavish interior, armoury, battlements and grounds are available, as well as displays and talks about the history of the castle and its famous occupants, not least Harry Hotspur himself.

All this ensures that the castle is presented in pristine condition. There are no crumbling ruins here. It's a highly organised visitor attraction. But if that's what it takes to preserve and maintain one of the most significant and important medieval castles in the country, then it's certainly a price worth paying.

The castle is located just off the main A1 road on the outskirts of the town of Alnwick. The main visitor entrance is at the end of Narrowgate, and parking is available on Greenwell Road and on Denwick Lane for the gardens entrance. Charges apply in these car parks. Other public parking and some on-street parking is available in the town itself only a short walk away.

Stewardship/Management – Privately owned and managed – Duke of Northumberland

www.alnwickcastle.com NE66 1NQ

Alnwick Castle Souvenir Guidebook – available on site or from the website

Admission: Charges apply; **Parking:** available close by - charges apply; **Scheduled Opening Times; Toilets; Café/Restaurant; Gift Shop; Exhibitions/Displays; On-site Management; Assistance dogs only; Disabilities:** Provision for disabled visitors, but some areas may not be accessible.

TWO

AYDON CASTLE

(otherwise known as Aydon Hall)

Located 1 mile north east of Corbridge, the castle is approached by way of narrow lanes off the A68 or the B6321 out of the town. Signs direct visitors down single tracks – this is deepest Northumberland. After a mile or so off the main road there is a small car park for visitors, and then a 200 yards walk along a farm-track that opens up to a view of the north-west curtain wall and the gatehouse. In a naturally defensive position, the castle stands on a bluff that drops steeply on three sides to the Cor Burn as it flows south-west towards its meeting with the River Tyne.

Set in woodland countryside Aydon is one of the finest and most unaltered examples of a 13th century English fortified manor house, and it's in remarkably complete condition. Originally built as an undefended residence, it was fortified on the outbreak of Anglo-Scottish warfare in the early 14th century. Pillaged and burnt by the Scots in 1315, seized by English rebels two years later, and again occupied by Scots in 1346, the castle eventually became a farmhouse in the 17th century and was lived in until as recently as 1966.

The land, on which a timber hall stood originally, was purchased by Hugh de Raymes, a wealthy Suffolk merchant, in about 1293. De Raymes expected to increase his social stature and influence by the acquisition of the property, but he did not live there. Eventually his son Robert took ownership and it was he who moved his household there and made Aydon Hall his primary residence. Robert is believed to have fought at the Battle of Falkirk in 1298 against the Scottish forces of William Wallace, and upon his return from fighting in Scotland he began the construction of the first stone structure.

Initially the manor did not feature any defensive works or fortifications, but in 1305 permission was granted to add crenelations[4] – defensive architecture on the battlements. These fortifications were probably status-driven at first, but proved a valuable defensive feature in 1311 as Scottish border raiders[14] began to launch incursions into English territory. Aydon itself was attacked during this time, successfully repelling at least two known assaults by Scottish forces.

Aydon's battlements - photo Ken Lussey

Following the Battle of Bannockburn in 1314 the English position became vulnerable, and Aydon Castle was captured by the Scots in 1315 after the governor of the castle surrendered. Aydon Castle was pillaged and severely damaged following the surrender and Robert de Reymes himself was taken prisoner. After being released on payment of a substantial ransom he returned to the castle to add further defences in the form of a curtain wall that secured the northern aspect of the property. However, Robert had been financially ruined by the ransom and the cost of repair to the castle. He died in 1324 with little to his name. By this time, the estate was considered worthless.

Ownership then came to Nicholas de Raymes who attempted to rebuild the previous fortunes that the family had enjoyed, but he was unsuccessful and was ultimately forced to sell. Aydon then changed hands a number of times with little change or physical alterations being made until the 17th century. From then onward, the castle was operated as a farmhouse. That use ended in 1966 when the property was opened to the public as a historic site which is now managed by English Heritage, and is recorded as a Grade I listed building

On approach to the castle the main gate is set into the curtain wall through which the outer courtyard gives onto the visitor reception and shop, while to the right the front wall carries on round past stone stables that are relatively modern. Directly ahead, running along the south side of the structure, is the heart of the castle. Another gate within a second defensive wall leads to an inner courtyard, with ranges of buildings beyond.

The grand, baronial interior of Aydon Castle

Photos Ken Lussey (above) and Simon Hawkins (right)

It's a high, solid stone building. Some is semi-ruinous but most is in an exceptional state of preservation. The visitor is able to wander around, both inside and around the outside of the castle, absorbing the atmosphere of the medieval world. The heavy stone walls, flagged and timber floors, a latrine block and crenelated parapets are well preserved. There are many original features – deep window reveals to narrow, arrow-slit windows, recesses, vaulted ceilings and fireplaces. In the upper floors is original timberwork, and a warren of rooms for banqueting, for defence and for retreat.

As very few changes were made in more recent centuries, the basic structure, layout and medieval features of the building have remained intact. As such Aydon Castle is of great historic significance. It offers a glimpse into what life must have been like in the turbulent times of the medieval era.

Fred Vincent

Stewardship/Management – English Heritage

www.english-heritage.org.uk/visit/places/aydon-castle/

NE45 5PJ

Souvenir Guidebook – available on site or from English Heritage
A narrated video is available at www.youtube.com/watch?v=cei_LZLXFd8

Admission: Charges apply; **Parking**: Charges apply; **Opening Times**: Scheduled summer opening times; **Toilets**; **Café**; **Gift Shop**; **Exhibitions/Displays**; **On-site Management**; **Dogs:** dogs on leads allowed; **Disabilities:** Provision for disabled visitors, but some areas may not be accessible

THREE

BAMBURGH CASTLE

Bamburgh's solid brown fortress grows almost naturally from the rock above the town with the handsome bearing of an old grandee. The great walls can be seen from miles away, imposing flanks towering above the road which curves beneath it past the wide, green cricket and recreation ground into the main, and pretty much only, street of Bamburgh.

The village is a spacious place with wide green verges, and a fork in the road encloses a village green with a canopy of oak, ash and sycamore. Cottages, small shops and a scattering of pubs line the road, but above it all the castle dominates the view. It is a staggeringly impressive sight.

Ron Lyons

The long volcanic crag on which the castle is built sits right above the sands and dunes that border the North Sea and has been occupied in one way or another since pre-historic times. In the 6th century the site of the castle was chosen by the Kings of Northumbria as their Royal capital and for many years it stood as a principal northern stronghold. As the castle faced persistent attacks by the Vikings between the 8th and 10th centuries and contests for power were fought out, the Northumbrian earls improved the castle's fortifications.

In 1066 William the Conqueror's invading forces spread northwards and his network of Norman barons and new nobility took control. As they did so in the far north defence against the Scots was imperative, and Bamburgh Castle became a strategic outpost. A mighty keep was erected - the same keep that exists today.

Photos Anne Nicholson (above) and Fred Vincent (below)

By the 15th century civil war brought Bamburgh into the spotlight during the Wars of the Roses[3] and the castle suffered badly, like Dunstanburgh just down the coast. Bamburgh became the first castle in England to fall to cannon fire. It continued to fall into further decline until, in 1610, the Crown, by James 1st, gifted the castle to Sir Claudius Forster, baronet and nobleman of Bamburgh, and for the first time it fell into private hands. It may be that King James passed the castle onto Claudius because he had been a loyal ally, but it has also been suggested that no one else was prepared to take on the eye-watering cost of repair and upkeep. Anyway, the main structure, the Norman keep, remained in good condition but the Forster family chose to live in the Manor House in Bamburgh, and the castle suffered further from lack of investment and maintenance.

In 1700 an heir of the Forster family, Dorothy, married Lord Nathaniel Crewe, the Bishop of Durham. When Dorothy died in 1716 the grieving Lord Crewe set up a charity with a view to restoring the castle and the fortunes of the people of Bamburgh. One of the pubs in the village is named after him today.

Bamburgh Castle painted in 1827 by John Varley (Metropolitan Museum of Art)

Lord Crewe's charity was a highly altruistic project, and the castle was used variously as a hospital, a school and a pharmacy. It worked for the benefit of the community and even had a spell as a coastguard and lifeboat station. The first lifeboat was commissioned by the Bishop's charity and launched from Bamburgh beach. The castle took in shipwrecked sailors and even paid for the funerals of those who lost their lives in the treacherous waters off the coast. However, although the charity carried out much in the way of building work and some restoration, and the setting was an active, lively community, the good Bishop's charity was unable to restore the castle fully. The bulk of its walls would have towered over the village, as it does today, but it was battle-scarred and forlorn.

The modern incarnation of the castle began in 1894 with Victorian visionary Sir William George Armstrong (he had been knighted in 1859 for his innovative development of the hydraulic engine and the rifled bore breech loading gun, the Armstrong Gun), Baron Armstrong of Cragside as he became known after being raised to the peerage in 1887. He bought the castle and surrounding estate for £60,000, and was to spend over £1 million renovating and restoring it all, a colossal sum at the time. Armstrong was born in Newcastle and although he was a trained lawyer, engineering, innovation and invention were at his heart. He was a pioneer of hydro-electric power and hydraulic systems. He developed engineering businesses and based them on the river Tyne. His companies became household names - Armstrong Whitworth built ships, locomotives and aircraft, Vickers-Armstrongs built planes and armaments, and Armstrong Siddeley built motor vehicles and aero engines. He was known as a philanthropist, a charitable benefactor, an environmentalist and an innovator. Such were his skills in engineering and invention that he received government commissions and his innovations in the field of hydraulics had far-reaching industrial benefits. He was a highly respected man.

Armstrong lived for a time in Jesmond, a suburb of Newcastle, where he designed and built the iron bridge over the dene there. He bought land near Rothbury north of Newcastle and built what was to become the great house and estate known as Cragside, where he constructed lakes and dams to create hydraulic and hydro-electric systems. His house was the first in the world to be lit by hydro-electric power. Cragside is now in the hands of The National Trust, an extensive domain of gardens, lakes and woodland.

Armstrong, and his descendants, came to Bamburgh and set about transforming it into his vision of the archetypal castle, housing his unique collection of artwork, ceramics and objets d'art that brought him great personal satisfaction. Now, long after his death but still in the hands of the Armstrong family Bamburgh Castle has become one of the most iconic, restored fortresses on any coast of England.

Sir William George Armstrong (Mary Lemon Waller)

The King's Hall - photo Ron Lyons

The present incumbents are his descendants Francis Watson-Armstrong and his wife Claire, the 5th generation of the Armstrong dynasty. Under their stewardship it has been developed into a major tourist attraction, a film location, and it offers itself as a venue for weddings, events and self-catering accommodation. It houses the Armstrong and Aviation Artefacts Museum which tells the story of William Armstrong and his inventions that contributed to legacies including the iconic Spitfire, Tower Bridge and the everyday lighting we have in all our homes. It tells the story of pioneering aviation history and Armstrong's innovations in areas encompassing air, land and sea.

The terrestrial and celestial globes, magnificent in their own right as both pieces of art and of practical application, are displayed in the Cross Hall, the centre-piece of the King's Hall. Made in the mid 19th century they epitomize William Armstrong's passion for art and technology combined. The celestial globe is richly decorated with astrological symbolism and its practical application was for seafaring and navigation purposes.

Impeccably presented, the interior features reflect the different ages of the castle's long life – from medieval stonework, roof and ceiling architecture and panelling to 18th and 19th century portraiture and even an early 20th century bakery. Visitors can explore the castle's staterooms accompanied by contemporary interpretations that bring to life its history and the people who have called it home. There's a very strong family connection here.

Within the great walls the castle site is wide and open with space to walk around the expansive battlements, cannon placements, and enjoy unrivalled views of the coast. The Farne Islands, Longstone lighthouse and the Holy Island of Lindisfarne can be seen from its commanding position 150 feet above the shore.

Since the 1960s the site has attracted much archaeological interest. Digs and excavations have revealed much information about the history of Bamburgh and its inhabitants and have confirmed the site's status as a Royal Citadel and seat of the Kings of Northumbria. The Bamburgh Research Project has been at the forefront of these investigations and their website records their work and findings.

The cannon displayed on the east battlement overlooking the coast are of the Crimea War period, or a little before it. They became redundant as artillery devices when shell ammunition replaced balls, and are displayed as a memorial to that time in the history of warfare.

The Norman origins of the magnificent keep at Bamburgh have been well preserved

Bamburgh castle has a great deal to offer the visitor on very many levels, from both ancient and modern history, valuable art and collections to highly entertaining and interesting exhibitions, displays and tours. Set in one of the most spectacular coastal landscapes to be found, Bamburgh is undoubtedly one of the finest restored castles in the country.

Stewardship/Management – Privately owned and managed – Armstrong family

www.bamburghcastle.com NE69 7DF

Bamburgh Castle Souvenir Guidebook – available on site or from the website

Admission: Charges apply; **Parking**: available close by - charges apply; **Scheduled Opening Times; Toilets; Café/Restaurant; Gift Shop; Exhibitions/Displays; On-site Management; Dogs**: in grounds only; **Disabilities:** Provision for disabled visitors, but some areas may not be accessible. Reduced rates, forward parking and shuttle service available.

Site-specific further reading:

- duchessthepodcast.com/episodes/claire-watson-armstrong-of-bamburgh-castle *[a 35 minute podcast in which Claire Watson-Armstrong speaks about the castle, its history, her family and all things Bamburgh]*
- bamburgh.org.uk *[an excellent tourist resource]*
- bamburghresearchproject.co.uk *[archaeological excavation project]*
- bamburghbones.org/lord-and-lady-crewe-a-1700s-love-story *[detail about Nathaniel, Lord Crewe and his wife Dorothy Forster]*

FOUR

BARMOOR CASTLE

Located some 5 miles inland of Lindisfarne on the B6353 outside the village of Lowick, the Grade II listed castle is today incorporated into a luxury, owners only, lodge and caravan park. There is no public access to the castle.

In about 685AD much of the land in the area was given to the Monks of Lindisfarne. When they re-settled in Durham following the destruction of the island's monastery, the land around 'Baremoor' was given to Durham Abbey. When the Normans arrived after the invasion of 1066 the Barony of Wooler with the Manor of Barmoor was given to the Muschampe family. A tower was built and a small town soon sprang up around it. Barmoor enjoyed royal and noble patronage, and hosted King Edward in 1291 and Edward II in 1319.

A licence to crenellate the tower[4] was issued on 17th May, 1341 by Edward III. There was much trouble between the English and the Scots at that time. Raids and attacks were frequent events. In 1417, Henry V and his Lord Wardens of the Marches assembled an army of 100,000 men at Barmoor to confront the Scots who had crossed the border. The Scots retreated at the approach of this formidable force.

However, the Borders continued to be the setting for many skirmishes between Scots and English, none more dramatic than the Battle of Flodden on September 9th, 1513. James IV of Scotland captured Etal, Ford and Chillingham before taking up position on Flodden Field. The English Army under the Earl of Surrey encamped the evening before battle at Woodend Wood, and spent the following evening at Barmoor celebrating their victory.

Over time the Border warfare took its toll and Barmoor suffered increasing damage and degradation. In 1541 a report lodged in Newcastle described the castle as *'ruinous and in extreme decay due to lack of repair'*.

In spite of the 1603 Union of Crowns[5] the border was still a hazardous place to live. The turbulent years drastically depleted the Muschampe fortunes and they experienced severe financial difficulties. Finally on 23rd February 1649, Lady Muschampe more or less gave up and renounced administration of her estates in favour of her husband's creditors.

In 1661 Barmoor then went to one of those creditors, William Carr Esq. of Etal and Gray's Inn, London. Over the decades Barmoor then passed through several hands until, at the end of the 16th century it fell to the Sitwell family. However, the Sitwells found it to be unsuitable as a family residence, and Francis Sitwell, in 1793, set about a total transformation. In 1801 it was rebuilt as a castellated Gothic-style country house, incorporating parts of the earlier castle. During the 19th century further modifications were made before the building was completed in 1892. It then enjoyed something of a revival and during the early 20th century was a significant and prominent family seat. It is said that in the 1960s the castle hosted a visit by Katharine Hepburn and Spencer Tracy when they were conducting a clandestine affair.

Today Barmoor Castle Country Park is a caravan and lodge park which is centred around the castle, owned and operated by the Lamb family who bought the castle and its estate in 1979, by then in a neglected condition. Major renovation of the site was undertaken before the first section of the park was opened in 1990. In 2010, a commemorative gate was built depicting the banners of the English Army, the Tudor Rose, typical weapons from 1513 and the Battle of Flodden, in recognition of the castle's history.

Stewardship/Management – Privately owned and managed

www.barmoorcastle.co.uk TD15 2TR

There is no public access to the castle.

Site-specific further reading: barmoorcastle.co.uk/history

FIVE

BEAUFRONT CASTLE

Located off the A69 between Corbridge and Hexham near the village of Sandhoe, Beaufront Castle is a privately owned 19th-century country house. It is a Grade I listed building.

The castle sits high above the valley of the River Tyne, commanding impressive views. It was first recorded as a pele tower[6] in 1415 and was the seat of the Carnabys in the reign of Elizabeth I. Dorothy Carnaby, heiress to the estate in the 16th century, married Gilbert Errington, and the Errington family built a new house in the 17th century.

During the 18th century the Erringtons spent a great deal of money on the gardens, plantations, lawns and hot-houses. At the end of the 18th century the house was demolished and the present house was built, designed by John Dobson[7], though it does include earlier remains. The kitchens and rooms above are 17th century and the clock tower bell is inscribed '1694'.

Beaufront Castle painted by J W Carmichael (1799 – 1868)

In 1810 the Rev. John Hodgson described the mansion thus: "*Few places make a finer appearance, or enjoy a larger and better cultivated prospect than this. From the south side of the Tyne it exhibits a long and handsome front surrounded with fine pleasure-grounds and from its walks are seen towns, towers, and hamlets and the winding stream of the Tyne, sometimes hidden under its banks and at others boldly crossing the meadows in broad and silver looking reaches*".

The property was acquired by the Cuthbert family in the early 19th century and the present imposing castellated Gothic revival style mansion was built, incorporating parts of the 17th-century house. William Cuthbert was High Sheriff of Northumberland in 1860.

It is recorded that on 31 January 1907 "*at Beaufront Castle, Hexham, the residence of Captain J. H. Cuthbert DSO. While a party was shooting over the grounds of the castle Captain Cuthbert slipped, and his gun exploded. The shot struck his wife, Lady Dorothy Cuthbert, and killed her.*" Captain Cuthbert married again but was killed fighting in the 1st World War. He had been a military colleague of John Kipling, the son of Rudyard Kipling, and it is said that Rudyard Kipling himself used to visit the castle after the war to talk to Cuthbert's widow about her husband's courage and his friendship with John.

Stewardship/Management – Privately owned and managed by the Cuthbert family

No website for this property NE46 4LT

There is no public access to the castle.

Resources and Further Reading
www.hexhamhistorian.org [*excellent archive photos*])

SIX

BELFORD

A castellated farmhouse sitting on the foundations of a 15th century motte and bailey castle, Belford Castle is situated just outside and to the north-west of the village of Belford. Sitting pretty much in the middle of a field it is now a privately owned house and part of a farm to which there is no public access. However, it can be viewed from the road and there is a footpath leading into the field right next to it.

Jane Brook

Mainly known as Belford Castle, it also goes by Belford Westhall Tower, Belford West Hall, Castrum de Belfurth or Castrum de Beleford. It is now part of Westhall Farm.

The castle was originally a Norman earthwork motte and bailey fortress. By 1415 it was described as having a strong, defensive stone tower surrounded by a moat, held by the D'Arcy family. It later passed to the Conyers, and then to the Forsters and Dixons, before being sold to William Clarke in the 18th Century. The presence of the later tower suggests this may have been a high status location.

The castellated Gothic farmhouse of today was built in 1837 on the earlier foundations of the castle.

Stewardship/Management – Privately owned and managed

No website for this property

There is no public access to the castle.

Resources and Further Reading
www.berwickfriends.org.uk/history/belford/ *[good detail of the history of Belford and the castle]*

SEVEN

BELLISTER

Situated just off the A69 road 12 miles west of Hexham and half a mile south of Haltwhistle on the south bank of the river South Tyne, Bellister Castle is a castellated 19th-century mansion house attached to the ruinous remains of a 14th-century tower house. It is now owned by the National Trust and is a Scheduled Ancient Monument and a Grade I listed building.

The National Trust acquired the property in 1976 and the Castle and Lodge have since been leased to tenants as a private residence. It is not open to the public, but can be viewed from attractive public footpaths that run through the adjoining woods.

Fred Vincent

The castle stands on a partly man-made mount - the earth structure of an 11th century motte and bailey castle. There is no trace of the moat that once surrounded it, and little remains beyond the earthworks and the earth mound of the motte.

From 1191 to 1295 a moated hall existed on the site, owned by Robert de Ros, an Anglo-Norman feudal baron, and his descendants. In 1312 it was acquired by Gerrald Salveyn, but confiscated from him in about 1354 - for reasons not recorded but he may well have in some way displeased the King at the time, Edward III. Displeasing the King in those days was never a good idea, and frequently resulted in attainment[12].

John de Blenkinsopp (*see the nearby Blenkinsopp Castle*) acquired it in about 1480 and built the tower which, in 1541, was recorded as being a bastell house (a term used for a high-quality building) in measurably good state of repair. In 1699 the property adjoining the tower was enlarged into a three-storey castellated house. A date stone confirms that date. The Blenkinsop family sold their estates including Bellister in 1697 and for many years thereafter the castle was held by several different owners.

By the early 18th century the tower had fallen into disrepair and one John Bacon bought the ruins in about 1715.

By 1818 it was in the hands of the Reverend Henry Westall, who had obtained the property through marriage. He sold it to John Kirsop of Wrexham. It was damaged by fire in 1827, after which the south eastern part of the house was rebuilt by the celebrated architect John Dobson[7] who applied his distinctive architectural style. Further re-modelling took place after a second fire in 1901.

Today the tower is a roofless shell, and in ruinous condition. Few original features of either the hall or the tower have survived. However some surviving architectural detailing, such as the moulded surround of a second floor window in the tower, and other moulded pieces lying loose within the ruin, suggest that this was a building of considerable status.

The following description of the property today is from the National Trust's manager for the Hadrian's Wall area: "*While the ruins are of a medieval castle, the home itself was converted into a mock-Gothic house by the famous architect John Dobson in the 1830s. It is a seven-bedroom family home which is a pocket-size castle. The castle is approached along a tree-lined drive and is surrounded by mature grounds including a walled garden, lawns, stables and an orchard. It also features grand reception rooms with wood-burning stoves and intricate ceiling mouldings, as well as a wide oak staircase, three bathrooms and an additional attic room*".

There is a very old Sycamore tree in front of the west side of the castle known as the 'Hanging Tree' where, during the Civil War, royalist cavaliers are reputed to have hung defeated Parliamentary troops. And to add to the dark side of the castle's history it is said to be haunted by the 'Grey Man' - the ghost of a minstrel who having been unjustly accused of being a spy was savaged to death by hounds as he fled the castle.

Stewardship/Management – National Trust

No website for this property NE49 0HZ

There is no public access to the property

Resources and Further Reading
visithaltwhistle.com/bellister-castle

EIGHT

BELSAY

The castle and the estate within which it is situated lies about 15 miles north west of Newcastle, 10 miles south west of Morpeth, off the A696 outside the village of Belsay. It is a Scheduled Monument and a Grade I listed building owned by the Middleton family since the 13th century and under the management of English Heritage since 1980.

Ron Lyons

The Belsay that visitors see today is made up of the old medieval castle, the much later Greek Revival mansion that replaced it as a family residence at the beginning of the 19th century, and outstanding gardens linking the two buildings.

The early origins of the site are in an Iron Age Hill Fort to the west of the present Belsay Castle. The Middleton family's links with the area were first recorded in 1270, when the estate of "Beleshou" was owned by Sir Richard de Middleton, King Henry III's Lord Chancellor. It is unclear what stood here at that time, perhaps a stone manor house and associated buildings, but it was obviously prestigious as King Edward I was hosted there in 1278.

In 1317 Sir Richard's grandson and heir, John, joined a local rebellion against the Crown, led by a cousin, Gilbert de Middleton. Both men were eventually captured and executed for treason. The Belsay estate was then forfeited to the state but in 1391 it returned to the Middleton family by marriage and since then it has remained in their possession. The family still own the estate today.

The existing fortified tower, which visitors can explore, is a substantial three-storey rectangular pele tower[6] with turrets and battlements. It was built in the late 14th century, probably added to the existing manor house. It is one of the best-surviving examples of a pele tower.

When the early 17th century brought relative peace to the border regions, local landowners like the Middletons rebuilt their houses with an emphasis on comfort and good living rather than defence, and at Belsay a mansion wing was added to the west side of the castle, converting it into a fashionable gentleman's residence. A plaque over the entrance porch gives a construction date of 1614. The builder was Thomas Middleton.

Ken Lussey

Thomas left Belsay to his son, Charles, but it would not be the family's main residence again until the 1670s, when Sir William Middleton, the 3rd Baronet, moved in with his second wife, Elizabeth. Finding the house by then in some disrepair he restored it and improved it further.

Sir William died in 1757 leaving large debts incurred as a result of opulent living and indulgences – wine, women and song as we might say today. His assets, including stud horses and the contents of the mansion, had to be sold off. The fortunes of the family were redeemed when his nephew William, the 5th baronet, married Jane Monck, the wealthy heiress of a London merchant who brought her wealth and restored the fortunes of the Middleton family.

In the late 18th century Charles, third son of Sir William Middleton, became the 6th baronet at the age of 16. The following year he changed his surname to Monck as a condition of inheriting the Lincolnshire estates of his wealthy grandfather, Lawrence Monck. Sir Charles, as he became, quickly established himself as a competent manager of the estate, and was given control of his own affairs even though still a minor.

Sir Charles had developed a passion for the Classics, particularly Greek, while at Rugby School, so when he married his cousin Louisa Cooke of Doncaster in 1804, they chose Greece for their honeymoon where they spent five months. While in Athens during the summer of 1805 Lady Monck gave birth to a son, Charles Atticus.

Once back in England Sir Charles Monck concentrated his attention on his estate and on county affairs. He indulged himself and his wealth by building a completely new Belsay Hall on a site several hundred yards to the south-east of the earlier castle.

The new Hall was completed towards the end of 1817, and on Christmas day Sir Charles and his family moved the short distance to their newly finished home, and in doing so they abandoned the castle as the family's residence. When Sir Charles died, aged 88, in 1867 his son Charles Atticus had already passed away in 1856, and so he was succeeded by his grandson Arthur, who in 1876 changed his surname back from Monck to Middleton.

Inside the tower the old rooms, passageways and vaulted ceilings are available to explore photo Ken Lussey

Although the new Hall at Belsay is a main feature for any visitor to the Belsay estate, the Hall is in all architectural and historical respects quite separate from the castle, and it is the castle with which this book is concerned.

Parts of the castle complex had been demolished by Sir Charles after moving his family into the new Hall, and Sir Arthur rebuilt the 1614 manor house which was attached to the castle to provide additional staff accommodation. He also reroofed it and restored the pele tower to its medieval form.

Sir Arthur planted masses of red, purple and white rhododendrons to create the rhododendron garden. He also added the winter garden with lawns for croquet and tennis, and the yew garden and magnolia terrace to add greater colour. The gardens comprise an intricate area of valleys and rockfaces fashioned from the quarrying which sourced stone for the new Hall, and a kitchen garden with heated walls.

During the Second World War the Hall was requisitioned by the Army and the gardens were not maintained. Furniture was stored in the attic, and the bedrooms and servants' quarters were occupied by soldiers. Nissan huts were put up in the service yard and grounds to house additional troops.

After the war the Middleton family moved back in and the castle and gardens were opened to visitors to bring in some extra income. However the Hall's sheer scale, combined with problems of damp caused by the system used by Sir Charles to avoid external drainpipes, meant that it was becoming an increasingly uncomfortable place in which to live. The ninth baronet, Sir Stephen Middleton, and his family, moved to a more manageable house, Swanstead, on the estate in 1962. Many of the contents of the mansion were sold off at auction, and dry rot began to infest the empty rooms.

The Hall, castle and gardens were taken into the guardianship of the state in 1980. There followed an extensive programme of repairs: wood and plasterwork was stripped out from many rooms in the hall and castle annexe to deal with the damp. The Hall is now displayed without furnishings as an empty shell, in line with the guardianship agreement, revealing to visitors the fine craftsmanship that went into its construction.

The formal gardens have been restored to their appearance in the 1920s and 1930s, while in the quarry garden Sir Arthur's exotic plantings have reached a magnificent maturity.

The 30 acre Grade I listed gardens that provide the magnificent setting for the castle and Hall are largely Sir Charles's work, and the layout has remained mostly unchanged since he set them out in the early 19th century - a serpentine drive and a lake with a cascade, exotic conifers, Scots pine and native hardwoods, a broad terrace walk with parallel borders of brightly coloured annual plants, a romantic quarry garden with its ravines, pinnacles and sheer rock faces, and one of the biggest collection of rhododendrons in the country.

Within the castle itself there is a maze of rooms to be explored, and 56 spiral stairs which lead to marvellous views from the top of the 14th-century pele tower.

The Baronetcy title became extinct on the death of the tenth Baronet, Sir Lawrence Monck Middleton, in 1999.

Stewardship/Management – The Middleton Family/English Heritage

www.english-heritage.org.uk/visit/places/belsay-hall-castle-and-gardens/

NE66 5NJ

Guidebook – available on site or from English Heritage

Admission: Charges apply; **Parking**: Free; **Scheduled Opening Times**.; **Toilets**; **Café/Refreshments**; **Gift Shop**; **Exhibitions/Displays**; **On-site Management**; **Dogs**: on lead only, no dogs in castle; **Disabilities:** Extensive provision for disabled visitors, but some areas may not be accessible.

Site-specific further reading:

www.historyofparliamentonline.org/volume/1386-1421/member/middleton-sir-john-1373-1441 (*a comprehensive biography of Sir John Middleton 1373 – 1441*)

www.parish-council.com/belsayparish/index.asp?pageid=407977 (*a history of Belsay*)

An Account of Belsay Castle in the County of Northumberland by Sir Arthur E Middleton - Published in 1910 by Mawson Swan & Morgan Ltd, Newcastle-upon-Tyne

NINE

BERWICK

There are two elements to the historic, military past of Berwick - the ruined remains of a medieval castle and the bastioned town defences - the mainly Elizabethan walls which surround the whole of the old town – walls which made the town itself the effective stronghold. Today their entire circuit can easily be walked providing a spectacular panorama over the town, the coast and the Tweed estuary with views south as far as the castles of Lindisfarne and Bamburgh.

Situated at the mouth of the River Tweed, the town of Berwick has a turbulent political and military past, having suffered centuries of conflict as control shifted back and forward between England and Scotland. The border now lies some 4 miles north of the town on a remote clifftop at a rustic wooden gate where a blue and white sign, the Saltire Cross of Scotland, marks the border between the nations. It has not always been so, and what follows demonstrates those centuries of war as English and Scots persistently battered the living daylights out of each other. One might be tempted to say that conflict between the two nations has, to some extent at least, continued into the 21st century with independence for Scotland being a constant and bitterly disputed political issue, but at least today those issues are largely contested by argument and debate, and not by the horrors of battle by sword and axe.

The broad walls present an opportunity for walks right around the town with vantage points and grand panoramas over the town and the coast - photos Fred Vincent

The border between two nations, marked by a simple gate and the white on blue Saltire Cross

However one looks at it though, the border has witnessed constant conflict for centuries, and as far as Berwick is concerned, being at the forefront of it all, each crisis brought repairs and improvements to the fortifications. While the castle itself has now fallen into ruinous disrepair, the great artillery ramparts – the walls which surround the town - survive largely intact.

The castle was commissioned by the Scottish King David I in the 1120s to protect the town's development as an important trading port on the east coast. Then, starting off what was to become something of a persisting contest, in the latter half of that century the Scottish king William the Lion tried to bring the whole of Northumberland under his control. In spite of much military melodrama he failed to do so, but it stirred things up and the English put their feet down, forcing William to concede Berwick to England in 1175 by the Treaty of Falaise. In need of cash to fund his Third Crusade in around 1190, the English King Richard then sold it back to Scotland. Even within the first 70 years it had all been back and forth three times.

Some crumbling walls survive from many centuries ago

In 1292, Edward I of England declared John de Balliol King of Scotland in Berwick Castle, but that was something of a false flag and on March 30th 1296 Edward's forces stormed its wooden walls during the First War of Scottish Independence. He subjected the townsfolk to cruel violence. The 15th century chronicler Walter Bower recorded: "*When the town had been taken in this way and its citizens had submitted, Edward spared no one, whatever the age or sex, and for two days streams of blood flowed from the bodies of the slain, for in his tyrannous rage he ordered*

7,500 souls of both sexes to be massacred...So that mills could be turned by the flow of their blood."

At the end of the 13th century and into the beginnings of the 14th the famous Scottish warriors William Wallace and Robert the Bruce both had their hands in resistance to English rule, and thus in the fortunes of Berwick. In 1297 Wallace led a rebellion and after success against the English at the Battle of Stirling Bridge, later in that year he mounted an attack on Berwick. Although he took the town the castle held out, and as the English garrison was strengthened, he was forced to withdraw.

The military barracks at Berwick – photo Ken Lussey

Eventually, in 1305 Wallace was betrayed, captured by the English and taken to London where he was put on trial for treason. He was convicted, sent to the Tower of London, stripped naked and dragged through the city at the heels of a horse to Smithfield where he was hung, drawn and quartered. His preserved head, dipped in tar, was put on a spike on London Bridge. His limbs were displayed, separately, in Newcastle, Stirling, Perth and Berwick. It is a gruesome example of public revenge and of what was considered deterrent justice at the time.

The following year 1306, somewhat courageously given what had happened to Wallace, Robert the Bruce led another rebellion against Edward I. This was successful and he was crowned King of Scotland. Edward's military response to this failed when Edward himself died, and over the next few years Robert strengthened his position throughout Scotland, although the English held out at Stirling and Berwick. Edward's son King Edward II raised a huge army and marched to confront the Scots, but he was heavily defeated at the Battle of Bannockburn by Robert the Bruce's far smaller army.

In 1315 Robert the Bruce had another go and besieged Berwick, and in 1318 determined to take this important sea port, he blockaded it from the sea, from where the town was being supplied and provisioned by the English. The Governor betrayed the town to the Scots, Berwick was forced to surrender and King Edward II was forced to retreat.

In 1333 King Edward III defeated the Scots at the Battle of Halidon Hill and recaptured the castle and town for England. Back to the English again.

Not prepared to let sleeping dogs lie, the Scots attacked again in 1355 and re-captured Berwick. But in an increasingly familiar scenario the English advanced and forced the Scots, yet again, to withdraw.

The Treaty of Berwick, signed in 1357, in theory put an end to the persistent border conflicts, but in reality it didn't. Not by a long chalk. In 1377 a combined force of Scots and French attacked. The English governor, much alarmed at the forces rallied at his doors, soiled his trousers and then killed himself by jumping out of the castle's upper windows. The castle was captured for the Scots. Again.

Henry Percy, Earl of Northumberland, then joined in the fray and took the castle back following an eight-day siege during which he killed the entire Berwick garrison. When, in 1384 he allowed the Scots to re-possess the castle King Richard II charged him with treason. He was pardoned after bribing the Scots into surrendering the castle back to the English for a large sum of money.

An engraving of Berwick Castle by William Miller (1796 – 1882) after J M W Turner

In the course of the Wars of the Roses[3] (1455–1487) Berwick Castle was granted to the Scots by the Lancastrian Queen Margaret of Anjou in 1461, in exchange for Scots support for the Lancastrian cause. However, in 1482 a Yorkist army led by Richard, Duke of Gloucester, recaptured Berwick for the Yorkist King Edward IV.

Thus Berwick, its castle and its strategically significant position, in 1482 were brought under English control for the final time. Over the course of a little more than 400 years, it had changed hands more than a dozen times, although it was not until the Wales and Berwick Act of 1746 that this position was finally enshrined in law.

After 1482 and the Yorkists' decisive occupation of the town for England, the borders still remained a place of some instability, and considerable repairs and strengthening of the castle's defences were undertaken. However, and although high walls and flanking towers like those which were built at Berwick were normally sufficient security against attack and damage from siege engines in the Middle Ages, the development of gunpowder artillery in the 16th century slowly reduced the value of traditional fortifications. In 1523 a survey of the castle concluded that its defences were insufficient to withstand cannon fire.

Berwick Castle barracks – photo Ken Lussey

As a consequence, the town defences were improved, including the building of a new three-storey tower on the river bank. Massive circular fortifications known as the Lord's mount were also erected. In 1558 Queen Mary of England ordered the medieval defences to be replaced with artillery bastioned fortifications. Bastions are gun emplacements projecting from the wall, enabling defenders to fire outwards across the ditch, and to repel an enemy attacking the walls to either side. The construction of the new fortifications became known as the Elizabethan ramparts. In 1558, a time of great tension between England and Scotland, these greatly effective defences rendered the actual castle obsolete.

In 1568 Mary, Queen of Scots, fled to England and as it became clear that King James VI of Scotland would succeed Queen Elizabeth I to become King James I of England, thus establishing the Union of Crowns[5], further defence was considered unnecessary and no further work was undertaken. The castle went into steady decline and in August 1590 a round tower used as the castle's only gun emplacement collapsed. Large parts of the structure were carried away for use elsewhere.

Although the castle continued to be garrisoned until 1603, in 1605 it was sold by King James I to the Earl of Dunbar who demolished much of the remaining building for its materials, and in 1611 upon the Earl's death, what was left passed to Theophilus Howard, the Earl of Suffolk.

Finally, in 1847, the Great Hall of Berwick Castle was demolished to make way for Berwick-upon-Tweed railway station.

As the function of Berwick as a fortified town diminished, in 1837 a pedestrian way along the ramparts was created, beginning their change of purpose from defence to leisure. It is now possible to walk the entire circuit of the town fortifications. The walls of the Elizabethan ramparts stand about 20 feet high, and above them the earthworks rise a further 16 feet. Outside there is a broad, deep ditch, or moat, now dry.

Against the southern rampart is the Main Guard, a Georgian guardhouse that once had a soldiers' room, a slightly more comfortable officers' room, and a prison cell for the detention of drunken soldiers, deserters, petty criminals and vagrants. It now contains an exhibition on the history of Berwick.

Ken Lussey

One of the access points onto the Ramparts is at Berwick-Upon-Tweed Barracks. Among the first barracks to be purpose built in England, they now house several historic exhibitions and in the summer host contemporary art installations. The Barracks have toilet facilities and a shop selling gifts, snacks and drinks

As one walks the walls today, all the notable elements of the ramparts and their ancillary structures are specifically named - Meg's Mount, Cumberland Bastion, Brass Bastion, Windmill Bastion, and the Powder Magazine - a gunpowder store surrounded by its own walled enclosure. There is informative signage on the walk, explaining the site's strategic importance and providing a detailed history.

Although very little now remains of the medieval castle, the ruins are fascinating to explore and there is

much to be seen on and from the walls around the town, not least the views of the stunning north-Northumberland coastline.

Stewardship/Management – English Heritage

www.english-heritage.org.uk/visit/places/berwick-upon-tweed-castle-and-ramparts

Guidebook – available online or from the gift shop

Admission: Free, Public footpaths accessible any reasonable daylight hours. The ramparts can be accessed at several points indicated by signage around the town; **Parking**: public parking around the town.; **Toilets** at Berwick Barracks; **Café/Refreshments** at Berwick Barracks; **Gift Shop**; **Exhibitions/Displays**; **Dogs**; **Disabilities:** There is disabled access to the ramparts. Due to the nature of the site, there are multiple sudden drops

Site-specific further reading:

www.discoveringbritain.org/activities/north-east-england/walks/berwick-upon-tweed.html (*detailed walk planner available here*)
www.visitberwick.com/what-to-do/walking/
www.historyhit.com/locations/berwick-castle/
MacIvor, I, 'The Elizabethan fortifications of Berwick-upon-Tweed', Antiquaries Journal, 45 (1965)

TEN

BLENKINSOPP CASTLE

Situated off the A69 about half a mile south of the route of Hadrian's Wall, 1 mile to the west of Haltwhistle, Blenkinsopp Castle is that rare thing – a castle that is also a pub. It's an old, ruined medieval fortified tower house and incorporated into those ruins now is a country inn, known as the Blenkinsopp Castle Inn. Although there is a modern car park and the site is closely surrounded by the chalets, motorhomes and static caravans of the residential country park, the ruins are quite well preserved and visitors are able to wander amidst it all. It is privately owned but access is freely available. It is a Scheduled Ancient Monument and Grade I listed building.

Records from the reign of Henry III (1207–1272) show that the land where the castle would later be built was owned by Ralph Blenkinsopp. The Blenkinsopp family constructed the substantial tower house there in about 1339. In view of the instability in the borders at that time a licence to fortify and crenellate[4] the house was granted on 6 May 1340. By the standards of the time it was likely to have been luxurious, as befitted an aristocratic family who owned much surrounding land, as well as providing a refuge for local, peasant families. Archeological research and old documents show that it had a moat, a great hall, a high-walled inner courtyard and defensive curtain-walling.

In 1541 the roof was found to be in decay and the tower in poor repair. The Blenkinsopp family abandoned the castle for their other property nearby at Bellister Castle, and later at Blenkinsopp Hall (formerly known as Dryburnhaugh, and a quite separate place to the site of Blenkinsopp Castle).

In 1727 the heiress to the Blenkinsopp estates, Jane, married into the Coulson family. The Blenkinsopp Coulsons, as they became, were mine owners and developed collieries nearby. The castle continued in poor repair and by about 1832 it was in disuse. The Blenkinsopp's colliery agent had a new house 'in the castellated style' built onto the east side of the ruins, thought to have been designed by John Dobson[7].

Between 1877 and 1880, William Lisle Blenkinsopp Coulson built a grand manor house on the site. Later in the 19th century the estates were sold to Edward Joicey whose family were also mine owners in the coal industry. It remained with the Joiceys for around 70 years, and there came a time during this period that the manor was converted into a hotel. Then, in 1954, a devastating fire gutted the building. The site was then acquired by the Simpson family, the owners of the residential home park. Some of the fire damaged ruins had to be demolished for safety reasons, but in conjunction with English Heritage much of the surviving stonework has been conserved.

In recent years, and with renovations to those parts that remained, it has been part home, part hotel, and part ruin. The old remains of the castle blend quite seamlessly, and somewhat incongruously, into the adjacent, renovated country inn. In 2015 the property was put up for sale, and the listing stated that "*one wing survived and now houses the family home, which sits within a larger residential park - also containing luxury chalets and Blenkinsopp Castle Inn*".

Relatively little original, medieval material now survives above ground. The position of the outer south wall and maybe a gatehouse probably lies beneath what is now a car park, and the area which now contains the inn had been the castle's coach stable.

For the benefit of visitors the ruins are well-supplied with information panels pointing out stonework from different time periods and features such as medieval carvings and re-used Roman stones.

Folk lore tells us that the castle is haunted by the "White Lady". The story goes that the avaricious, medieval lord Bryan de Blenkinsopp married a rich, foreign wife. She possessed a chest of gold so heavy that it took 12 men to carry it, but she refused to tell Bryan where she kept it. He went off to search for it and was never heard from again. His wife, stricken with remorse, went to look for him, and she, too, was never heard from again. Legend has it that, tortured by her actions, she was doomed to haunt the castle as the White Lady.

Stewardship/Management – Privately owned

www.blenkinsoppcastleinn.co.uk/ CA8 7JS

Toilets, refreshments and the usual facilities are available in the pub

ELEVEN

BOTHAL

WELBECK

Situated in the village of Bothal off the A197, about 10 miles north of Newcastle and 2 miles west of Morpeth, Bothal Castle is a castellated stately home near the river Wansbeck. It is part of the Welbeck Estate, a Scheduled Ancient Monument and a Grade I listed building.

Simon Hawkins

In 1095, King William Rufus, William II, third son of William the Conqueror, gave Bothal to Guy I de Balliol. His daughter Alice married William Bertram, Baron of Mitford, who built a hall house on a low spur above the river in about 1150.

Several generations later, in 1343, Sir Robert Bertram was given permission to castellate his manor house, including a licence to crenellate[4]. The works he carried out included an impressive gatehouse, and a good deal of the medieval gate tower and fragments of curtain wall still survive to this day. Through the marriage of Bertram's daughter Hellen to Sir Robert Ogle the estate passed to the Ogle family in the 14th century.

For more than 200 years the castle passed through various hands, family feuds and legal wrangles, but it remained in good condition and in 1576 it is recorded that the castle had, among other facilities, a great chamber, seven bed chambers, a bakehouse, a brewhouse and its own prison.

In 1591 the estate passed to the Cavendish-Bentinck family (the Dukes of Portland). It is recorded that King James visited on 5 May 1617 on his way to Scotland and stayed for two nights.

Derek Taylor

Restoration work was carried out in the 19th century when the castle was incorporated into a new house built in the 1840s. The rest of the castle was built within the last sixty years.

Fred Vincent

Bothal Castle is a stunning, picturesque castle located close to the road and river, and is in an excellent state of repair. The ruined curtain walls, 3 feet thick and up to 14 feet high and the gatehouse with its portcullis in perfect condition, are stunningly impressive. Today the building is owned by the descendants of the Cavendish-Bentinck family, and the offices of the agent of the Duke of Portland, all forming part of the Welbeck estate. Views of the castle can be obtained from vantage points in the surrounding countryside, but no unauthorised public access is permitted to the estate.

Stewardship/Management – Privately owned: Parente/Cavendish-Bentinck family; Welbeck Estate

No dedicated website

NE61 6SL

Resources and Further Reading:

Bothal Observed: A Survey of a Northumbrian Castle, Village and Church – Roland Bibby, 1973

TWELVE

BYWELL CASTLE

Bywell Castle is situated in the village of Bywell overlooking the river Tyne, four miles east of Corbridge. It is a Grade I listed building and a Scheduled Ancient Monument. The castle is in the grounds of a private residence.

Bywell Castle pokes discreetly through the parkland and presides over the river Tyne

The castle stands on the north bank of the Tyne where an 11th-century Norman castle was built by Guy de Balliol around 1090. By the 15th century the Manor of Bywell was in the hands of the Neville family and in about 1430 Ralph Neville, the second earl of Westmorland, improved the old, Norman fortifications by adding a curtain wall and gatehouse. It was intended to be part of a larger castle, but this was never fully completed.

King Henry VI fled to Bywell Castle after his defeat at the Battle of Hexham in 1464. His enemies were close behind, and when Lord Montague arrived at Bywell he found the king's crown, helmet, and sword, but Henry had gone, becoming for a time a fugitive in his own lands until his brief return to the throne on 3 October 1470. They were complicated times, and a period of breathtakingly complex political shenanigans, and in all this Bywell appears to have played some small part.

Following the involvement of Charles Neville, 6th Earl of Westmorland, in the Rising of the North[8] the Neville estates were forfeited and Bywell was sold in 1571 by the Crown to the Fenwick family. William Fenwick built a new house at Bywell next to the old partially completed castle, to designs by architect James Paine in 1760.

The estate was sold to Thomas Beaumont early in the 19th century and the house was improved. Alterations were made to designs by John Dobson[7] in 1817, in 1827 and further extensions were added in the 1890s.

The castle gave its name to a ship built in 1869 at Jarrow. The SS Bywell Castle was involved in an accident when she collided with the paddle steamer the SS Princess Alice on the river Thames in September 1878. The Princess Alice capsized and sank with the loss of more than 600 lives. Although both vessels

Bywell Castle by Walter Scott (1814)

were initially held responsible for the collision the Bywell Castle was eventually found blameless.

The castle is now private property, the seat of the Beaumont family, the Viscounts Allendale. The present occupiers, the 4th Viscount Wentworth Beaumont and his wife Vanessa, have carried out significant improvements to the 18th century hall that adjoins the castle, and operate the estate's business of property and farming as well as hosting events such as the Northumberland County Show, the Bywell Horse Driving Trials and supercar event Bella Auto.

Today, the impressive three-storey gatehouse remains, together with part of a curtain wall, but apart from very occasional garden open-days, the property is not open to visitors. Due to its location is difficult to view, especially in summer when the foliage of the grand trees that surround it obscure much of the view. However, good glimpses of it can be had from the roadside and the nearby churchyard.

Stewardship/Management – Privately owned

No dedicated website

NE43 7AB

Resources and Further Reading

There are a number of websites and resources dedicated to the collision between the SS Bywell Castle and the steamer Princess Alice
northcountyshow.co.uk/

THIRTEEN

CARTINGTON CASTLE

Cartington Castle is a ruinous, medieval English castle in the hamlet of Cartington, 2 miles north-west of Rothbury and two miles north of the village of Thropton, looking down on the River Coquet. The ruins now sit next to working farm buildings and a small cluster of cottages. It is a Scheduled Ancient Monument and a Grade I listed building.

The site's first recorded owner was Ralph Fitzmain in 1154. In the late 14th century a pele tower[6], the original " Tower of Kartyngton", was built, probably by John Cartington. In 1442 Cartington was granted a licence to crenellate[4] and extended the existing tower, adding a courtyard, a great hall, and a tower-defended courtyard.

Brian Tait

By Cartington's endeavours the castle became a fully defensible position. As a mark of its significance Margaret, Queen of Scots, with her baby daughter, stayed here on her flight from Scotland to London in November 1515, having travelled from nearby Harbottle Castle. On several occasions the castle hosted troops en-route from one bust-up to another.

In 1541 the castle was described as being a good fortress of two towers and other strong stone houses in good repair, owned by Sir Cuthbert Radcliffe. In 1601 Sir Francis Radcliffe gave it to his son in law, Roger Widdrington.

During the Civil War[2] the castle was a Royalist centre held for the King and, as a consequence, was besieged by Parliament forces. In 1648 Sir Edward Widdrington raised 2,000 soldiers and 200 horse to withstand the siege, but after some brief resistance it was eventually taken and deliberately put beyond defensive capability[9]. The castle was later partially dismantled and the stones used to build outhouses, walls and barns.

Despite that partial demolition, the castle continued to be occupied until finally abandoned in the 1860s. In 1883 Sir William Armstrong, Baron Armstrong of Cragside as he became known, bought it and secured the structure to prevent its complete disintegration.

Fred Vincent

The castle was a much greater, grander and strategically important property than the current remains suggest. Even so, the ruins are quite extensive and on the ground it's plain to see that the original fortification was a walled enclosure with a tower at each corner. The early layout was interrupted before it could be finished, and the north-east turret was replaced by a fortified tower house. This tower house formed the core of the medieval castle.

At the eastern side of the castle site is a small rectangular courtyard. There are turrets at the north-east and south-east corners. The northern turret is only partially complete but the southern turret still stands and includes a garderobe – a toilet chute. At the south-west corner stand the ruins of a tower destroyed in the Civil War siege.

The northern side of the courtyard is occupied by a complex of buildings - a 14th-century tower, a great hall and secondary chambers, mostly in ruins. The position of large windows inserted into the great hall during the Tudor period are still apparent, and at the south-west corner are the remains of a stair turret.

Cartington Castle is on private land, though it is easily visible from the surrounding country and from the road through the village. It is possible, discretely, to approach the ruins over the fields or through the farm and explore them. There is no on-site supervision or management and care should be taken on the stones and uneven surfaces.

Nearby is the estate of Cragside, the house built by William Armstrong before he moved to establish his ancestral seat at Bamburgh Castle.

Stewardship/Management – Privately owned

No dedicated website

NE65 7JW

Resources and Further Reading

Upper Coquetdale, David Dippie Dixon, 1974 (*record of archeological excavations*)

FOURTEEN

CHILLINGHAM CASTLE

The intact, Grade 1 listed, medieval castle is situated in the hamlet of Chillingham, parish of Chatton, off the B6438, 8 miles south west of Bamburgh. In addition to the castle itself, a number of structures within the grounds are listed Grade II. These include the West Lodge, gateways and garden walls. A pair of urns in the Italian Garden are similarly listed.

Originally there was a monastery on the site of the castle in the late 12th century, and in medieval times a fortified, moated manor house occupied this strategically important location on the border between the two feuding nations of England and Scotland. It was used as a staging post for English armies heading for Scotland, and was repeatedly attacked and besieged by Scottish armies and raiding parties heading south.

In 1296 a Scottish raid destroyed the manor house, which was replaced by a tower house forming one of the four corner towers existing today. King Edward I visited Chillingham in 1298 when on his way north to confront William Wallace at the battle of Falkirk.

Chillingham Castle – front entrance

A licence to crenellate[4] was granted to Sir Thomas de Heaton in 1344, upon which Chillingham was effectively upgraded to become a fully fortified castle, complete with dungeons and torture chambers. It was built in quadrangular form with great towers at the four corners, a style rarely found in Northumberland, and which forms the basis of what can be seen at the castle today.

From the rear gardens *Ron Lyons*

From the 15th century Chillingham has been the seat of the Grey family. For their services to the country, especially in the wars against the French, they were made Earls of Tankerville, and given other prestigious titled positions. However, some eight executions for high treason recorded within the family archives suggest that they didn't always choose their loyalties wisely.

Chillingham suffered significant damage during the years of the Pilgrimage of Grace[10], a popular revolt beginning in Yorkshire in October 1536 before spreading to other parts of Northern England, which probably resulted in the rebuilding of some of the towers. It was refurbished and redeveloped in Tudor and Stuart times. At its centre is the Great Hall, an Elizabethan chamber overlooked by a medieval minstrel gallery.

As relations between the two countries became rather more peaceful following the Union of the Crowns[5] in 1603 and being united by a single sovereign, the need for a military stronghold in the area declined. The castle was gradually transformed - the moat was filled, and battlements were converted into residential wings. A banqueting hall and a library were built.

In about 1824 Capability Brown re-landscaped the grounds. Extravagant gardens and avenues were laid out by Sir Jeffry Wyatville who had been celebrated for his work in the restoration of Windsor Castle.

During the Second World War, the castle was used as an army barracks, and during this time much of the decorative wood was stripped out and burned by the soldiers billeted there. After the war, the castle started to fall into disrepair. Lead had been removed from the roof, resulting in weather damage to large parts of the building and before long, with disuse and declining security against the elements, the castle fell further into ruin. In 1982 it was bought by Sir Humphry Wakefield, 2nd Baronet, whose wife Katherine was descended from the Greys of Chillingham. Sir Humphry began a careful restoration of the castle.

The castle courtyard has fine, original architectural detail with its ballustrades, fine stone staircase, crenellation and heavy stonework. From here the visitor can explore the opulent rooms, the collections of artifacts and even the torture chamber

Throughout the centuries the castle's architectural detail and massive walls have remained largely intact, and Sir Humphry sought to retain and preserve much of the ancient, historic fabric of the building. The medieval strength and character of the castle remain.

Having taken on the dilapidated castle in 1982, Sir Humphry stripped it back to its medieval roots and filled it with an eclectic collection of furniture and objects, from mantraps to elk's antlers. The numerous rooms contain many original pieces, from opulent drawing rooms filled with paintings and tapestries to torture chambers with the most gruesome instruments of horror - most of them still in perfect condition. Today's visitor will find balustraded galleries, a museum, a library, and the grand Great Hall with its stone flagged floor, tapestries, armour and weapons. Trophy antlers of deer and wild cattle hang from the walls. Long dining tables are laid with the paraphernalia of an opulent age.

Such is its impressive grand and original styling, in 1997 the castle was used as a filming location for Elizabeth, featuring as Leith Castle and as the hunting lodge. The mock fireplaces from the film which replicate the 16th century structures remain in the great hall, covering the later white marble ones from the 18th century.

The Great Hall (above) and the Torture Chamber (right)

Darren Chapman

Outside, the formal gardens and woodland walks are all fully open to the public. The work of designer Sir Jeffry Wyatville includes a famous herbaceous border said to be the longest in northern England, a jousting grandstand and views of the surrounding countryside with the grand scenery of the Cheviot Hills. There are lakes, wildlife and woodland. Deer, squirrels, foxes, rabbits and badgers live in the woods along with an abundance of bird and plant life.

The 300 acre park adjacent to the castle is famous for its wild white cattle – said to be the same animals that were used for Roman sacrifice. Although the cattle are now under the care of an independent foundation, they are a unique breed and an important part of the castle's history. The cattle have lived at Chillingham since a park wall was erected in 1220, and perhaps for long before that. In medieval times the animals were hunted, but today they live freely. They are never handled, anything other than the most necessary intervention being avoided.

Sir Humphry Wakefield's family have lived on the same lands in the Lake District for 400 years, just half the length of time the Greys have lived at Chillingham and their other surrounding castles. The Hon. Lady Wakefield is daughter of the former Lady Mary Grey from nearby Howick Hall, and from the historic Chillingham family line.

Sir Humphry, educated at Gordonstoun and Cambridge University, was a Captain in the 10th Royal Hussars. His biography tells us that he is a lifelong horseman and has lived a life of travel, adventure and the Arts. He is an art dealer, historian, adventurer, even a rodeo rider and army tent-pegging champion, so we are told. He is President of the Northumbrian Mountain Rescue teams, of the distinguished Northumbrian Avison Ensemble, and of other charitable concerns. He is Chairman of the international Wilderness Foundation and Director of the Tree of Life Foundation. He is a Fellow of the prestigious American Morgan Library and of the British Royal Geographical Society.

The castle is said to be the most haunted castle in Britain and a little micro-industry has developed around this reputation. Television presentations have featured the ghosts of Chillingham Castle, not least in an episode of the Most Haunted T.V. show. Late night ghost tours are put on for those visitors willing to experience the dark recesses of the castle's shadowy past.

The Italian Gardens

Although there are many stories of one ghostly apparition or another, the most famous is the "Blue Boy", who is said to torment visitors to the Pink Room. The guests who have claimed to have sensed his presence are said to have witnessed flashes of blue or a halo of blue light over their beds, and heard a terrifying lament. The glowing figure was then supposed to manifest itself as a little boy dressed in blue. Terrifying. Other sinister discoveries within the castle walls include the bones of a man and a boy found within a wall 3 metres thick. Remnants of mouldering blue fabric were discovered along with the skeletons.

For those wanting more time to explore the castle and the exceptional surrounding Northumbrian countryside and coast, self-catering apartments are available at all times of the year, which includes free access to the castle grounds. Some apartments to let are in the actual castle, and some in the castle's nearby Coaching Rooms

Stewardship/Management – Privately owned, Sir Humphry Wakefield

www.chillingham-castle.com NE66 5NJ

Guidebook – available on site

Admission: Charges apply; **Parking:** Free; **Opening Times:** April – November 11.a.m. – 5.00.p.m.; **Toilets**; **Café/Restaurant**; **Gift Shop**; **Exhibitions/Displays**; **On-site Management**; **Assistance dogs only**; **Disabilities:** very limited disabled access. The castle may not be suitable for anyone with mobility difficulties, due to uneven floors and steep spiral staircases. To access the toilets and tearoom, spiral stone steps with a rope handrail also need to be negotiated

Site-specific further reading:

Chillingham: Its Cattle, Castle and Church, Paul Bahn, 2016

FIFTEEN

CHIPCHASE CASTLE

The castle is situated in the parish of Chollerton, some 30 miles north west of Newcastle, ten miles north of Hexham. It lies on the east bank of the North Tyne, a mile or so downstream from Wark and about ten miles upstream from Wall.

The property is described as a large, impressive 14th century Tower House with a later 17th-century Jacobean mansion built alongside. It is widely regarded as one of the best preserved towers and of exceptional architectural and archaeological importance. It is a Scheduled Ancient Monument and a Grade I listed building.

Courtesy Chipchase Castle/Jonathan Elkington/Neil Denham

The 4 storey stone-built tower has a vaulted cellar and watchtowers at each corner, linked by a crenellated parapet walk. The medieval portcullis is still in place. There is limited public access to both the tower and the mansion.

Unlike many of the significant estates Chipchase has not been in the same family for centuries. It has, over the years, been in and out of various ownerships, often for reasons of financial insecurity or failure of some sort. The castle's website gives a detailed account of how the estate devolved since it was first developed by the Insula family in the 13th century down to its present owner Jonathan Elkington, an international property and wealth manager, and descendent of the Taylor family who have owned the estate since the mid-19th century.

The area surrounding Chipchase was occupied as early as the Bronze Age, but its first recorded mention is in the thirteenth century when it was acquired by the Insula family - a name that probably has its derivation in the Roman word for communal living. In 1261 Sir Peter de Insula obtained a licence to strengthen his mill dam on the North Tyne – a reflection of the border tensions at the time. Sir Peter's descendant, Cecily, married Walter Heron in 1367 and the Heron name became one of the principal family names in the history of the castle, retaining possession of Chipchase for over 350 years.

Courtesy Chipchase Castle/Jonathan Elkington/Neil Denham

In 1490 John Heron was appointed Bailiff of Rededale with attendant duties to "*capture felons and evil-doers*" and bring them to justice. However, he seemed to have been in continual financial wrangles of one sort or another and it is said that the Herons were hot-tempered, regularly in trouble with the authorities and had many enemies.

They must have calmed down a bit over the years because in 1625 Cuthbert Heron became High Sheriff of Northumberland. He built the fine Jacobean mansion that stands today, attached to the original tower. Cuthbert's first son George, a Royalist in the service of King

Charles I, was killed at the Battle of Marston Moor in 1644. His second son, also Cuthbert, was created a Baronet by Charles II.

The Heron family managed to remain in possession of the Chipchase estate until 1727 when more financial problems eventually led to the sale of the estate to George Allgood, a lawyer who belonged to a family that had for some generations been at the forefront of civic life in Hexham, although he seems to have been always at odds with his tenants and neighbours, and a rather unpopular man.

George Allgood died in 1728, and the Chipchase estate was sold to John Reed of Bellingham, a Newcastle upon Tyne banker, in 1734. John Reed died in 1754 and was buried in a chapel which he had built at Chipchase. He was succeeded by a nephew, Christopher Soulsby of Newcastle. Soulsby assumed the name of Reed and became High Sheriff of Northumberland in 1764. He died in 1770 and in 1823 his son John Reed was financially ruined by the failure of the family bank Blake, Reed and Co, and his estates, including Chipchase, passed to trustees for the use of creditors.

Courtesy Chipchase Castle/Jonathan Elkington/Neil Denham

The trustees sold Chipchase to the Greys of Backworth in 1826. Ralph William Grey lived at Chipchase for most of his life, during which he was M.P. for Tynemouth amongst other civic and charitable positions. In 1862 Grey sold the estate to Hugh Taylor whose family descendants own Chipchase to this day.

When Hugh Taylor passed away, Chipchase passed on through Taylor family heirs, eventually passing to Lt Col Thomas George Taylor, who lived there in 1945, then to Lt Col Richard Ian Griffiths Taylor who died in 1984. The property then passed on to his daughter Penelope and then to her son Jonathan Elkington who currently owns and runs the estate.

Today the castle is deliberately not commercialised. Jonathan Elkington's aim is to safeguard the estate for future generations, and he feels strongly that he is a custodian of its heritage, and of his family heirloom. His intention is to leave it in as good, or better, condition for future generations to enjoy. Jonathan has worked hard as an entrepreneur and private equity investor, has personally managed and farmed his estate at Chipchase, engaging in forestry, fishing and shooting, which enables him to preserve the heritage and history of Chipchase he so strongly values. The castle is open to the public on limited occasions, usually for one month during the year.

Stewardship/Management – Privately owned and managed; Jonathan Elkington

www.chipchasecastle.com NE48 3NT

There are limited on-site facilities other than for those attending specific events

Ashley Lightfoot

SIXTEEN

DILSTON CASTLE

Dilston Castle is a ruined 15th-century tower house situated in the village of Dilston, about a mile south-west of Corbridge. It is a scheduled monument and Grade I listed building. The castle is in the grounds of Dilston College and is not accessible to the public other than by prior arrangement. The Northumbrian Jacobite Society occasionally arrange group visits, and their very comprehensive website [*www.northumbrianjacobites.org.uk*] provides information about this and much else about the history of the Jacobite association and the Radclyffe family.

The 15th century three-storey fortified tower house was built by Sir William Claxton on the site of an earlier pele tower[6]. It was built with a barrel-vaulted basement, gun-loops and a four storey extension.

The claim to the Dilston estate was contested by the Tynedales who took it by force in about 1430 with support from the powerful Percy family. Sir Robert Claxton recovered possession in 1441. Years later the Radclyffe family, who originated in Lancashire, succeeded to the manor of Dilston and the tower by the marriage of Edward Radclyffe into the Dilston family.

Fred Vincent

In 1616 Sir Francis Radclyffe had been suspected of complicity in the Gunpowder Plot, but he was not long detained and when he succeeded to Dilston he began work on extending the tower and the construction of a chapel close by. A new manor house, which was to become known as Dilston Hall, was incorporated into the tower.

During the Civil War[2] in the 17th century the property was forfeited to the state, but reverted to the Radclyffe family at the Restoration[11] of the Monarchy to Charles II in the 1660s. The Radclyffes were created the Earls of Derwentwater and in 1709 James Radclyffe, the 3rd Earl, began a program to replace the old Elizabethan/Jacobean manor house with a substantial Queen Anne mansion. This new mansion was never completed as he was convicted of treason and executed in 1716 for his part in the Jacobite rising of 1715. The ghost of his wife is reputed to haunt the castle.

As a result of his treasonous behaviour the 3rd Earl was attainted[12] as was the succession of his heirs, and the estate was forfeited to the Crown. The subsequent attempted disposal by the Crown authorities was mired in so much irregularity that the estate was eventually, and by much legislative connivance, possessed by the Greenwich Hospital for its benefit.

The estate remained in the hands of Greenwich Hospital and the mansion, which had been left uncompleted on the execution of the 3rd Earl, was demolished in 1765, leaving standing only the castle tower and the chapel.

In 1865 the Hospital Commissioners transferred the property to the Admiralty Board, who sold it in 1874 to Wentworth Blackett Beaumont, 1st Baron Allendale - industrialist, Liberal politician and mine owner.

A restoration of the buildings took place in 2001, funded by the Heritage Lottery Fund, and included work on the roof, repointing, the construction of a new timber floor, and a staircase to access the upper levels. The tower nevertheless remains in ruinous and uninhabitable condition.

Dilston Castle and Chapel are situated in the private grounds of Cambian Dilston College, an independent specialist provider of further education for young people with a learning disability, Autism Spectrum Disorder and complex needs. Access is possible only by prior arrangement with the college authorities.

Stewardship/Management – Privately owned; Cambian Dilston College; MENCAP

No dedicated website

NE45 5RJ

No public facilities are provided on site

Site-specific further reading:

- www.northumbrianjacobites.org.uk/
- History of Corbridge and Its Antiquities; With a Concise History of Dilston Hall; Robert Forster; 2016
- Dilston Hall: Or Memoirs of James Radcliffe, Earl Of Derwentwater, A Martyr In The Rebellion Of 1715; William Sidney Gibson; 2010

SEVENTEEN

DUNSTANBURGH CASTLE

1 mile north of the coastal village of Craster, access to the imposing ruins of Dunstanburgh Castle is on foot only, by a grassy, clifftop path from the village to the south, or along Embleton beach from the north.

One of only two castles actually perched on the coastline of Northumberland, along with Bamburgh, Dunstanburgh is perhaps the most evocative, atmospheric ruin to be found anywhere. Its remote, exposed position and its stark, solid stonework reflects the centuries of conflict to which it has been witness.

Fred Vincent

The castle sits on the headland formed by the northernmost outcrop of the Great Whin Sill, a layer of igneous rock featured through the counties of Cumbria, Durham and Northumberland. Hadrian's Wall takes advantage of its high, rocky outlines, and here at Dunstanburgh in the 13th century it offered a promising defensive location, although as it turned out not an impregnable one.

The view from Craster to the spiky ruins of the castle is iconic. The road around the harbour passes in front of a row of white cottages, most with the rosettes and window stickers of the tourist rental, and then ends at a gate which leads onto the grassy path to the castle. In season the line of shorts and sunhats snakes along the clifftop path like a cinema queue.

Ron Lyons

Ken Lussey

The castle is quite inaccessible by vehicle, save perhaps for the 4x4s of English Heritage who are currently charged with its upkeep. The walk along the grassy, sheepy, clifftop path brings Dunstanburgh ever closer, looming larger with every step until standing beneath the massive gatehouse one can imagine its powerful influence in days gone by.

The spiky ruins are perhaps reminiscent of the eccentric shapes left by the World Trade Centre towers, its outline against the sky a clear depiction of conflict and war. But unlike the grim consequences of 9/11 these ruins possess a romantic, stirring spirit, a place resonant of knights in armour, heraldic pennants, heroic deeds and bravery. In its ruinous condition it manages to maintain an almost majestic defiance. One can imagine the cries and chaos of battle, the clang of sword on shield and the thump of cannon. Yet in spite of this faux romanticism the battles which took place here were just as brutal and just as ill-conceived as the atrocity perpetrated against the citizens of the United States in 2001.

Ruined it may be, but the brown stones rise dramatically above as the path takes the visitor around its feet. The great gatehouse, towers and battlements have withstood the storms of this coast for hundreds of years, but they could not withstand the assault and battery occasioned by the conflict between the Yorkists and the Lancastrians during the Wars of the Roses[3] in the 15th century. It was so badly damaged that the castle fell into disrepair and was derelict soon afterwards, never to be restored.

Simon Hawkins

It's a huge site, although not obviously so from the approach. In its heyday the great walls enclosed a full 10 acres which held a market, housing, barracks, supplies and all the offices of living and for the administration of the lands around. Now only some exterior walls, the great gatehouse and a tower known as Lilburn tower remain amongst the stones and low ruins of ancillary buildings. Nevertheless, its dramatic, distinctive silhouette against the skyline can be seen for miles up and down the coast. Today it's a place to wander about and imagine the past, the remoteness of the place and the transience of power and war set against a backdrop of unassailable, unconquerable nature.

The site was probably first occupied in prehistoric times. A promontory fort with earthwork defences was built on the same location at the end of the Iron Age, possibly being occupied into the Roman period. By the 14th century, the defences had been long abandoned, and the land was being used for arable crops.

In 1269 Henry III granted an estate here to his younger son Edmund, Earl of Lancaster, who built the castle between 1313 and 1322 – a response to the English disaster at Bannockburn. Edmund's son, Thomas, became an immensely powerful English baron, the second richest man in England after the King, with major land holdings across the kingdom. He took advantage of the site's natural defences and the existing earthworks of the Iron Age fort, intending it as a secure refuge and a statement of his wealth and influence.

A licence to crenellate[4] was issued by Edward II in 1316, and the resulting castle was huge, protected on one side by the sea, with a stone curtain wall, a massive gatehouse, and six towers around the outside. A harbour was built on the south side of the fortress, for supply or escape by sea as the case may be. Northumbria was a lawless region in this period.

Thomas was a powerful opponent of King Edward. He resented the favouritism shown by the King to certain members of his court - in particular to Piers Gaveston upon whom the King had bestowed much privilege and titles. It was even suggested that the King and Gaveston were lovers. Piqued by all this Thomas ordered Gaveston's execution, for which King Edward was unable to forgive him.

Derek Taylor

Thomas was also an unpopular man, especially locally. He angered his tenants by increasing taxes to pay for his ambitious building program and the huge cost of maintaining his personal army. At a time when harvests were failing, famine was rife and sheep and cow disease were at epidemic proportions, Thomas's men continued to take advantage of their employer's powerful position to extort their way into private fortunes. With the King unable to intervene, the North of England became effectively under Thomas Lancaster's control.

However, Lancaster was unable to make much use of his seat and probably only visited his new castle once. Suspected of being in league with the Scots and pursued by the King's forces, in 1322 he was captured at the Battle of Boroughbridge as he attempted to flee royal forces for the safety of Dunstanburgh. Thomas was executed, and the castle became the property of the Crown. King Edward considered it a useful fortress for protection against the threat from Scotland.

By his marriage to Henry of Lancaster's granddaughter in 1362, Dunstanburgh Castle came into the hands of John of Gaunt. Gaunt was the 3rd son of King Edward III and, as the Duke of Lancaster, was one of the wealthiest men of his generation. He expanded Dunstanburgh's defences in the 1380s in the light of the threat from Scotland and the peasant uprisings of 1381.

Ken Lussey

Gaunt further expanded Dunstanburgh's defences over the next two years, but over time he lost interest in it. Dunstanburgh Castle remained part of the Duchy of Lancaster, but the Duchy was annexed to the Crown when Gaunt's son, Henry IV, took the throne of England in 1399.

Henry VI inherited the throne in 1422 and during the next few decades while the castle maintained a strategic northern stronghold in the region, numerous repairs were undertaken to the buildings and outer defences, which had fallen into disrepair. The Wars of the Roses[3], a dynastic conflict between the rival houses of Lancaster and York, broke out in the middle of the 15th century and saw the castle changing hands between the rival Lancastrian and Yorkist factions several times.

As a Lancastrian stronghold the castle was defended by Sir Ralph Percy, a man of somewhat wavering allegiances. In September 1461 he surrendered it to the Yorkists. In 1462, Henry VI's wife, Margaret of Anjou, invaded England with a French army, landing at Bamburgh. Percy then switched sides back in favour of the Lancastrians. In response the Yorkists besieged the castle and Percy, knowing what was good for him, surrendered. He was left in charge of Dunstanburgh as part of Edward IV's attempts at reconciliation, but the next year he once again switched sides, returning the castle to the Lancastrians.

The castle was badly damaged during the wars and never really recovered. It was assaulted, battered, sieged, and had cannon fired at it until it fell to bits. Other than minor repairs in 1470 it fell into disrepair and has lain in ruins ever since. It was used as a base for piracy in 1470 and its roof robbed for lead. By 1538 it was described in a royal report to Henry VIII as "*a very ruinous house and of small strength*", and it was observed that only the gatehouse was still habitable. Some repairs were carried out but in 1543 it remained in very poor condition.

In 1550 the castle was described as being "*in wonderfull great decaye*". Alice Craster, a wealthy widow, occupied the castle from 1594 to 1597, probably living in the gatehouse, where she carried out some minor restoration work, and farming the surrounding estate. For much of the 16th century, local farmers used the outer bailey of the castle to store their cattle in the event of Scottish raids.

From Embleton Bay – the spiky ruins record a prominent position on the headland

In 1603, the unification of the Scottish and English crowns[5] eliminated any residual need for the castle as a royal fortress. The Scottish border became more stable and the military significance of the site steadily diminished. In 1604 King James I finally sold the dilapidated property off into the private ownership of Sir Ralph Grey, a nearby landowner. Ralph's son, William Lord Grey, is recorded as the owner of the castle in 1625.

The Grey dynasty maintained their ownership of the castle, but the site reverted to a more local, sustenance use. The lands around were used for growing wheat, barley and oats, and the stones of the great walls were taken for other building work. During the Grey family's ownership it fell increasingly ruinous, and became a popular subject for artists, not least the celebrated J. M. W. Turner.

The estate was later sold to Sir Arthur Sutherland, a wealthy shipowner, in 1919. However Sir Arthur could not afford to maintain it, and he placed it under the guardianship of the state in 1930.

In the Second World War, measures were taken to defend the Northumberland coastline from a potential German invasion. The castle itself was occupied by the Observer Corps, and the surrounding beaches were defended with lines of barbed wire, slit trenches, a minefield, weapons pits and reinforced concrete pillboxes to the north and south of the castle.

In its medieval landscape the castle was surrounded by three artificial lakes called meres. With its 10 acre enclosure it was the largest castle in Northumberland. The most prominent remaining part is the Great Gatehouse, a massive three-storey fortification. Multiple rectangular towers protect the walls, including the Lilburn Tower, and the Egyncleugh Tower. Three internal complexes of buildings, now ruined, supported the earl's household, the castle constable's household, and the running of the surrounding estates. Of the harbour that was built to the southeast of the castle, only a stone quay survives.

In the 21st century, the castle is owned by the National Trust and managed by English Heritage. It is a Grade I listed building and a Site of Special Scientific Interest. It is now a perfect place to wander around, wonder at the history, listen to the cries of seabirds wheeling in the wind and gaze at the stupendous scenery of the Northumberland coast.

Features: The Keep and the Great Gatehouse; Lilburn Tower; the curtain walls; the Constable's Tower and Egyncleugh Tower; Picnic areas; walks including Embleton Beach

Stewardship/Management – National Trust; managed by English Heritage

www.english-heritage.org.uk/visit/places/dunstanburgh-castle/ NE66 3TT

Guidebook – available on site or from English Heritage

Admission: Admission Charges to the castle – surrounding areas are free to walk around; **Parking**: No vehicle access. Paid parking is available in Craster; **Scheduled opening times**; **Toilets** none on site; **Limited refreshments**; **Gift Shop**; **On-site Management** during opening hours; **Dogs** on leads; **Disabilities:** Access path grassy but uneven; on site ramps but uneven surfaces and stairs

Site-specific further reading:

- Dunstanburgh Castle (English Heritage); Alastair Oswald and Jeremy Ashbee; 2007

EIGHTEEN

EDLINGHAM CASTLE

Edlingham Castle is situated beside The Burn, a tributary of the Aln, in the hamlet of Edlingham off the B6341 6 miles south-west of Alnwick. The fortified manor house guarded one of the few approaches to Alnwick through the hills to the west, an important function during the period of unrest in the borders. It is a Grade 1 listed building in the care of English Heritage. Public access is freely available but there are no on-site facilities or management.

The property dates from about 1295 when William de Felton bought an earlier, wooden manor house from the Edlingham family. Felton was a member of an important family with estates in Norfolk and Shropshire but he had made his fortune independently through military service, royal favour and by way of marriage to a Northumberland heiress, Constance de Pontop. The Feltons became a prominent family dynasty in the history of the castle.

Simon Hawkins

William rebuilt the house in stone. It had two storeys with vaulted cellars and a great hall above with octagonal turrets at each corner. There was a variety of service buildings within the courtyard, including a kitchen, brewhouse and bakehouse. In about 1340 an opulent solar tower[13] was built and as the Anglo-Scottish wars continued a gatehouse and curtain wall with battlements were added to complete the defences. At the end of the century, the gate tower was enlarged, and the walls strengthened. The castle became an imposing structure, a symbol of manorial wealth and power.

In 1514 it was purchased by George Swinburne, a constable of Prudhoe, but by the end of the Civil War in the 17th century the castle had become derelict, and by 1661 the buildings were being used as a source of building stone. Today, and apart from the solar tower, only the low stones remain, and the rampart that once surrounded the manor survives only as an earthwork.

The best preserved part of the castle is the solar tower, although even that is quite ruinous and parts lean at a precarious angle. The north and west walls of the tower survive almost to the full height of its 3 storeys. The first-floor room has a double line of windows and the remains of an elaborate fireplace.

The site is easily accessible on foot from the nearby village church of St John the Baptist. William de Felton is buried there. An information board is on-site, and leaflets are available from the church for a small donation.

Ken Lussey

Stewardship/Management – English Heritage

www.english-heritage.org.uk/visit/places/edlingham-castle

NE66 2BW

There are no facilities on site. There is a small, free parking area. The castle is open at any time.

Site-specific further reading:

- Edlingham Castle: the military and domestic developments of a Northumbrian manor; Fairclough, G.; 1982

NINETEEN

Northumberland
National Park

ELSDON CASTLE

In the village of Elsdon, about 10 miles to the southwest of Rothbury, the earthwork remains of Elsdon Castle are the best preserved medieval motte and bailey castle site in Northumberland. In the absence of any structures above ground, the area is often referred to as the Mote Hills.

There is evidence of settlement in the area from prehistoric times. The Romans also left their mark, but it was with the Normans that Elsdon found its place on the map. In 1076, only 10 years after the Norman invasion, a charter granted the Lordship of Redesdale to Robert de Umfraville, Lord of Tours and Vian, a close ally of William the Conqueror. The Normans were keen to secure their grip on northern England in the decades following the Conquest, and much of it was given out to supporters and relatives of the first Norman king. The Lordship occupied a strategically important route between Newcastle and Edinburgh, critical to defence against Scottish raids.

A bird's-eye view of the motte & bailey earthworks — *Fred Vincent*

The Umfravilles became a powerful dynasty in Redesdale. They appointed judges, exercised justice, were allowed to hold fairs, and were granted the right to hunt in royal forests. They were the law in Redesdale.

Robert de Umfraville, also known as "Robert with the Beard", built the castle in about 1076. It was originally built as a circular motte on the natural spur of a hill, topped by a timber fortification. The bailey below the motte was protected by an earthen bank and ditch, with a timber palisade on top of the bank. The original wooden structures were partly replaced in stone in the early 1100s.

The castle fell into disuse after Henry II regained Northumberland from Scotland in 1157. The Umfravilles were granted new lands a few miles to the north where they built Harbottle Castle, moving their seat there from Elsdon. With no longer a role to play, Elsdon gradually fell into decline and was eventually abandoned, no longer mentioned in estate records by 1245.

An artist's impression of how the motte & bailey may have looked at Elsdon

The site is freely open to the public. It consists of a 15-metre high and 80-metre wide tall mound or motte to the south, with an embanked crescent-shaped bailey to the north. There are no obvious walks around the site and it is a steep climb up to the top of the twin mottes. There is a public information board on site.

Stewardship/Management – Northumberland National Park Authority

No dedicated website NE19 1AB

Free parking at the roadside. There are no on-site facilities or management

TWENTY

ETAL CASTLE

Etal Castle is a ruined medieval fortification in the village of Etal, close to the border with Scotland some 8 miles south-west of Berwick. It's a fine example of a small castle in what was a wild and dangerous region, where cross-border raiding and warfare were common during the Middle Ages.

Set above the south bank of the River Till, the ruins comprise a curtain wall 3 feet thick and 25 feet high surrounding a large courtyard. The south side is almost complete and the west only in fragments. Little else of the walls remain. A tower within the courtyard, a tower house at the north west corner and an impressive gatehouse complete the picture. Today it is set within manicured lawns framed with fine trees that provides an attractive setting for visitors exploring its history.

The gatehouse at Etal

Ron Lyons

Following the Norman invasion of 1066 the means of keeping control of the subject population was by the creation of baronies – large tracts of land given to a powerful warrior lord to administer. Each barony was subdivided into manors, which were governed by knights loyal to their baron. The resources of the land financed the system and enabled it to function and profit. In return, the baron and his knights defended the border and gave military service to the king. The manor of Etal lay within the barony of Wooler, created for Robert de Muschamp in 1107. The barony extended in a broad continuous block across Northumberland, from the Cheviot Hills in the west to the North Sea at Budle Bay in the east. By 1232 Etal was owned by Robert Manners.

Manners built the castle in around 1341 after he was granted a licence to crenellate[4] by King Edward III in order to defend the location against the Scots. The Manners family had owned the manor since at least 1232 and the castle was probably built on the site of an older, unfortified house owned by the family. By the 1350s, the castle was well-developed, fortified and surrounded by a manor which included corn-mills, lime kilns and coal mines.

Simon Hawkins

Unruly and belligerent behaviour was not confined to border wars between England and Scotland. The Manners were involved in a long-running feud with the nearby Heron family, who owned the neighbouring Ford Castle. On 20 January 1428 there was a fight between the two sides outside Etal Castle, in which William Heron died.

By 1438 the castle, then in the hands of another Manners descendant, Robert, had fallen in value considerably as a result of the wars with the Scots, the feuding with the Herons and the poverty of the lands. In 1495 another Manners descendant, George, inherited the title of Baron de Ros from his mother's side of the family and the castle was abandoned as a family residence around the end of the 15th century when the Manners moved closer to the royal court.

In the absence of the Manners, Etal Castle was managed by the Collingwood family, who eventually became the castle's hereditary constables. The castle still formed an important strategic defensive location and was heavily involved in the border wars with Scotland.

August 1513 saw the Battle of Flodden Fields. James IV of Scotland invaded England with a large army equipped with modern artillery. He took the border castles of Norham and Wark, and then moved south against Etal. Etal surrendered quickly in the hope of avoiding being pillaged by James' army, but nonetheless it was slighted[9] - deliberately damaged to prevent it being used as a defence.

After the English victory at the Battle of Flodden, the castle was retaken, garrisoned and used to store captured Scottish artillery. The castle was continuously used for one thing or another in the early 16th century, until in 1541, a royal commission reported that the castle and its buildings were "*in very great decaye*".

The battle of Flodden exhibition at Etal Castle

Ken Lussey

The Crown bought the castle from the Manners in 1547 and installed a garrison. Although in poor condition the castle remained important to the defence of the border, but without investment in maintenance and repair it fell further into disrepair - in 1564 it was described as "*scant able to lodge the captain*". After the Union of Crowns[5] in 1603 it lost its military value and was abandoned as a fortification, passing into private ownership. In the 18th century it ceased to be used even as a domestic dwelling and became ruinous.

An impression of how the castle at Etal may have looked in the 14th century with the gatehouse and crenellation complete, and much activity within the walls

In 1908 the long-abandoned Etal Castle was acquired by James Joicey, 1st Baron Joicey, a coal-mining magnate, and by 1922 the ruins had been cleaned of ivy and given preventative maintenance to protect against further degradation. The castle was placed into the guardianship of the state in 1975 and now, still owned by the Joiceys, is managed by English Heritage. Open to the public, it is a scheduled ancient monument and a Grade I listed building. The site includes an award-winning exhibition about the battle of Flodden. Access, including for those with disabilities, is through the shop.

ENGLISH HERITAGE

Stewardship/Management - Joicey Family; Ford & Etal Estate; English Heritage

www.english-heritage.org.uk/visit/places/etal-castle

TD12 4TN

Guidebook – available from English Heritage

Admission: Free; **Parking**: Free; **Opening Times**: Seasonal/Scheduled opening times; **Toilets** in village; **Picnic Area**; **Dogs** on leads; **Disabilities:** Disabled access paths but some undulating ground

TWENTY ONE

FEATHERSTONE CASTLE

The castle lies 2 miles south-west of Haltwhistle on the south bank of the river South Tyne. It is a large, fortified Gothic style country mansion and a Grade I listed building. Now in private hands it functions as an events venue with hostel-style accommodation and is not open to the casual visitor.

The earliest recorded history of the area is from the Roman occupation period. Hadrian's Wall, which lies about 3 miles to the north, was constructed during the 2nd century.

In the 11th century the manor was at that time part of the barony of Langley under Scottish rule. The first recorded owner was Helias de Featherstone in 1212. The Featherstonehaugh family retained ownership for several centuries, during which it played an important role in the border conflicts between the English and the Scots. Originally a 13th-century hall house, a square three-storey pele tower[6], protected by a moat, was added in 1330. In 1541 the property was reported to be a tower in good repair, occupied by Thomas Featherstonehaugh.

The Royalist Sir Timothy Featherstonehaugh was executed at Bolton in 1651 following his capture at the Battle of Worcester, and the castle was confiscated by parliament. It was then sold to the Earl of Carlisle but the Featherstonehaugh family bought it back in 1711, only to sell it on in 1779 to James Wallace, the Attorney General. Wallace's crest, a lion, is much in evidence at the castle.

James' son Thomas Wallace carried out further alterations between 1812 and 1830, and bequeathed the estate to his nephew Colonel James Hope who changed his name to Hope-Wallace to honour the legacy of his uncle.

In the early 1940s a training camp for American troops was built beside the river at Featherstone. This was shortly afterwards repurposed as a camp for Italian prisoners of war, and German Officers. Between 1945 and 1948 some 25,000 Germans were housed there in compounds surrounded by barbed wire and watch towers. In 1945 the watch towers and barbed wire were removed and voluntary labour outside the camp, workshops and political or cultural courses were encouraged. The camp was a highly regarded example of the rehabilitation of prisoners and British-German reconciliation. Remains of the camp survive today as foundations and a scattering of brick buildings in the parkland.

The property was sold in 1950 and became a boys' preparatory school, known as Hillbrow School. In 1961 the school moved to new premises, and Featherstone Castle passed hands again ultimately to the present owner who operates it as a residential conference and activity centre.

Photos Fred Vincent

Like many places with a history of medieval shenanigans Featherstone has its ghost stories, and a strong following of people exploring the paranormal. Legend has it that in the 17th century Abigail Featherstonehaugh was to marry a neighbouring Baron's son, but was actually in a lovers' tryst with another, a local called Ridley. As the bridal party rode the bounds of the estate, the spurned Ridley attacked them, but the new bridegroom put up a fight. It must have been quite a fracas as everyone was killed. One assumes, perhaps, that the last man standing must have fallen upon his own sword. Anyway, at midnight the sound of horses' hooves was heard outside the castle, and when the door opened into the banqueting hall the ghostly apparition of Abigail and the rest of the party entered, clearly showing the terrible wounds that had been inflicted upon them. The Baron had no stomach for this sort of thing and fainted. It is said that the ghostly wedding party can be seen each 17th January in Pynkin's Cleugh, a narrow valley just over the river from the Castle.

The various alterations to the structure over the centuries have resulted in a large castellated and complex country house. It is well-preserved and presents an impressive feature in this part of the Northumberland landscape. The castle and its substantial grounds are now owned by Colonel John Clark, and is available for group bookings, as a venue for wedding receptions and gatherings of that sort, and of course for those keen to witness the ghostly goings on in the darker hours in this beautiful old building.

Stewardship/Management – Privately owned

www.featherstonecastle.com NE49 0JG

Whilst the castle is private property, there are excellent views from the road and surrounding country. There seems to be no reason why it can't be approached, discreetly, for a closer look.

There are no facilities provided for the casual visitor.

TWENTY TWO

FORD CASTLE

The castle is to be found some 10 miles inland west of Lindisfarne, 15 miles south of Berwick. It's about 3 miles south-east of Etal Castle and part of the Ford and Etal Estate owned by the Joicey family.

Ford is a Grade I listed building situated at a shallow crossing point at the village of Ford on the river Till. Ford was simply named from a ford across the river, though today there is a bridge. The castle and its grounds are currently operated as a young persons' activity centre and not open to the public, but there is probably no reason the casual visitor cannot approach it from the exterior grounds for a closer look at the beautiful buildings beyond the portcullis gate.

Simon Hawkins

There has been a settlement on the site of Ford Castle since Anglo-Saxon times. In the 13th century, the land was granted to Odinel de Ford who built a manor house here. Following his death it was acquired by the Heron family, a name which will be familiar to those who have already taken a look at the history of nearby Etal Castle. Sir William Heron was granted a licence to crenellate[4] in 1338, and Ford Castle was recognised as part of the border defences. As a result of this, however, the castle has been raided, sacked and burned many times during its long and tempestuous history.

Convivial neighbourly relations do not seem to have been high on their agenda, and the Heron family's reputation seems to have been one filled with deceit, murder, betrayal and more than one bitter feud.

Amidst their belligerence the Scots prevailed, and the castle was captured and dismantled in 1385, but later repaired by William Heron who was not to be deterred. However, in 1388 he was arrested and taken to Newcastle where he was imprisoned. Ford Castle was taken, and the garrison massacred.

The Herons refused to accept defeat and by the beginning of the 16th century Ford had been rebuilt and refortified. Indeed, it was a suitable place for King James IV to establish a headquarters as he was heading south towards England to invade in 1513. Having set up base at Ford Castle he delayed there for a few days, a decision attributed to his downfall. It is thought that his delay may have been occasioned by his infatuation with the reputedly beautiful wife of William Heron, and this rather took his eye off the battle plan. Although Lady Heron did not reciprocate she was anxious to please, motivated by the desire to protect her home and secure the release of her husband imprisoned in Scotland.

James' romantic dalliance may have cost him though, as the delay gave the English time to prepare for the forthcoming Battle of Flodden. The Scots suffered a crushing and humiliating defeat, and James IV was killed. The Scots retreated back north, but before they left they burned and destroyed the castle.

Eventually, the castle passed from the Herons to the Carr family by marriage in 1549, but by 1584 the castle was in a ruinous state and by royalist action in 1648 it was rendered untenable. The property then passed to Sir Francis Blake of Oxfordshire, by marriage in the 1660s.

In 1694 Blake built a substantial mansion in the Tudor style within the castle walls. On Blake's death in 1717 the Ford estate passed to the husband of his late daughter Mary who had married into the Delaval family, and then in 1723 to her son Francis Blake Delaval. Classically, aristocratic family marriages, mergers and liasons resulted in the amalgamation of several family names at Ford. The Waterfords, Delavals and Blakes all had their hands in the devolution of the estate. Eventually it passed to Susannah, Marchioness Waterford. In 1862 Louisa, Dowager Marchioness of Waterford, widow of the 3rd Marquess, restored and substantially re-modelled the Hall.

In Seaton Sluice, on the coast towards the southern boundary of Northumberland, both the Waterford Arms and the Delaval Arms bear witness to the connection between the two families and their association with both Ford Castle and wider communities.

The union of the Blake and the Delaval families is said to have resurrected a curse, which warned that the Delavals and the two families should never be joined. If they were, the curse declared, no Delaval man would die peacefully in his bed. It is claimed this curse took the lives of nine male Delavals, and eventually that of Sir John Hussey Delaval who died at his breakfast table in 1808, no doubt by a surfeit of lampreys, or an excess of one thing or another.

The castle was acquired in 1907 by the coal-mining magnate and Liberal MP for Chester-le-Street James Joicey, 1st Baron Joicey, who also purchased Etal Castle and the Etal estate. During the Second World War the castle was used as a hospital by the British Red Cross and St John's Ambulance. In 1956 the Joiceys leased it to Northumberland County Council which established it as a Young Persons' Residential Centre.

The council withdrew in 2016, and in 2022, Ford and Etal Estate agreed a 26-year lease with PGL who now operate the site as an outdoor activity centre for schools, groups and young people. PGL takes its name from its founder in the 1950s - Peter Gordon Lawrence. The company's stated aim is to create safe, stimulating environments where young people have the freedom to discover, learn and explore.

The castle now, under the management of PGL, offers accommodation for primarily school-age children accompanied by teachers or under similar adult supervision. The children have the benefit of the castle's amenities, organized activities, the grand halls, elegant rooms and artefacts which tell the stories and the history.

Simon Hawkins

Although the castle is not open to the public, the footpath from Ford Village offers views of the portcullis gateway and the grand exterior.

Stewardship/Management – Privately owned and managed – Joicey family/Ford & Etal Estates/PGL

www.ford-and-etal.co.uk/history-heritage/ford-castle/

TD15 2PX

There are no facilities provided for the casual visitor.

TWENTY THREE

HALTON CASTLE

The castle is located just off the A68 2 miles north of Corbridge. It is a 14th century pele tower with a later 17th century manor house attached and is the private residence of Sir Hugh and Lady Blackett. It is a grade I listed building and is not open to the public.

Halton itself is an extraordinary little place. Well off the beaten track it's an approach down narrow, leafy lanes to a dead-end. It can't even be described accurately as a village, as there's nothing there except for the attractive house with attached castellated tower, a church and a small collection of cottages. Oddly, there's a post-box installed in a wall.

The hamlet is remarkably manicured, with wide, closely-mown green verges, and because it's a no-through road it's very peaceful and quiet. The views over the Tyne valley are nothing less than spectacular.

The tower was first recorded in 1382 and it is still present today. It has four storeys and a basement with a stone vault. A manor house was added onto the north side in the 15th century, but much of that building was demolished by the then owner John Douglas in about 1696. He replaced it with the present five-bay residence, in part using masonry from a nearby Roman fort.

In 1751 Anne Douglas the heiress of Halton married Sir Edward Blackett, a baronet and member of the House of Commons for Northumberland. He was the sole heir of Oley Douglas, whose father had acquired the estates of the once powerful Carnaby family. This brought Halton Castle into Blackett ownership.

The terraced garden has those stunning views overlooking the Tyne valley, herbaceous borders, lawns and shrubs with massive beech hedges. Open garden days are held occasionally.

Stewardship/Management – Privately owned and managed – Blackett family

www.theblacketts.com/node/160 NE45 5PH

TWENTY FOUR

Northumberland National Park

HARBOTTLE CASTLE

The ruined remains of this medieval castle are found at the village of Harbottle about 8 miles west of Rothbury, overlooking the river Coquet. It is a Scheduled Ancient Monument and a Grade I listed building, managed by the Northumberland National Park Authority.

The mound on which the keep stands was probably a site used by the ancient Britons. The present castle was built about 1160 when Henry II ordered Odinel de Umfraville to build a castle at Harbottle. The Umfravilles were relatives of William the Conqueror and great Lords of Coquetdale and Redesdale to whom William awarded large swathes of Northumbria to defend against the enemies of England. The castle at that time would have been a simple motte and bailey enclosure, forming part of a chain of such sites across the region as protection against the Scots.

The site of Harbottle Castle, above the village. The winding river Coquet lies below the camera
Fred Vincent

Not long after its construction however, in 1174, the Scots mounted a successful attack and took the castle. It was then strengthened with stone.

In 1296, it was besieged by the feudal baron Sir Robert de Ros, but the siege was successfully resisted. In 1318 Robert the Bruce took the castle and by 1336 it had been again restored and strengthened. Lack of interest and investment saw it fall into ruins again by 1351. Yet again, at the end of that century it was repaired and in about 1436 the castle passed into the hands of the Tailleboys. It became the residence of the Warden of the Middle Marches, a particularly wild part of the borders, and used as a prison.

Simon Hawkins

In 1515, Margaret Tudor, the widowed queen of King James IV of Scotland and sister of King Henry VIII of England, came to the castle with her second husband, Archibald Douglas, 6th Earl of Angus. There, their daughter, also Margaret, was born, who became the mother of Lord Darnley, husband of Mary, Queen of Scots and father of King James VI of Scotland and, upon the Union of Crowns[5], James I of England.

In 16th century the castle underwent various re-building and restoration work and in 1605, King James I granted the castle and manor to George Home, 1st Earl of Dunbar and Lord Treasurer of Scotland. Thereafter the castle fell into decay and much of its masonry was used

in other buildings, particularly in the construction of a new 19th century manor house. This was located at the east end of Harbottle village and re-used the name Harbottle Castle.

The Sad Castle Memorial Stone
Who made me into a ruin like an old city?
Was it the soldiers who rode out on horseback?
Was it my old enemy the Scots?
Or was it those border reivers?
Perhaps it was just the centuries passing.

Felicity Lance 1997
A pupil of Harbottle School
stone carved by David Edwick

A survey of 1715 reported the castle to be ruinous once more.

The castle has experienced a surprisingly frequent cycle of repair and ruin, reflecting the unpredictability and uncertainty of those times. Today, only earthworks and some standing masonry remain. The motte is over forty feet high and is surrounded by a ditch 6 feet deep. Parts of the curtain wall still survive. The site is freely available to the casual visitor and only a short walk out of the village. There are no visitor facilities at the site and only very limited facilities in the village, but the situation and the surrounding countryside make Harbottle Castle an attractive place to visit and wander through the stones which mark such a fascinating period of English and Scottish history.

Stewardship/Management – Northumberland National Park Authority

www.northumberlandnationalpark.org.uk/places-to-visit/coquetdale/harbottle

NE65 7DG

Admission: Free; **Parking**: Free in the village; **Opening Times**: Unlimited

Site-specific further reading:

www.harbottlecastle.co.uk/index.php [*a site maintained by the Friends of Harbottle Castle, and an excellent information resource*]

TWENTY FIVE

HAUGHTON CASTLE

Haughton Castle is an imposing, privately owned fortified country mansion and Grade I listed building, situated to the north of the village of Humshaugh on the west bank of the North Tyne, around 5 miles north of Hexham. It is not open to the public.

Situated in what can only be described as the middle of nowhere, the castle is approached by winding, narrow lanes. It's a highly discreet estate and access to any part of it which might afford a view of its imposing façade is unavailable to the public, other than those prepared to risk a challenge of trespass. For those who, one way or the other, manage to find a viewing point it is hard to imagine a more striking, impressive building which one can only imagine must have commanding views over the surrounding, wooded countryside of Northumberland.

The castle was built in the 13th century, originally as a tower house, then enlarged and fortified in the 14th century by the addition of turrets, battlements and parapets. At this time the castle was owned by Gerald Widdrington, and although the Widdrington family continued to own it for several centuries, it was frequently tenanted and in the early 14th century it was occupied by the Swinburn family.

By the 16th century the castle seems to have been falling into disrepair and an attack by border reivers[14] in 1541 resulted in the theft of horses and property. The castle was significantly damaged and was abandoned as a residence, a report of the time stating that the roof and floors were "*decayed and gone*".

The ruinous property was acquired by the Smith family in about 1640, but no major improvements were carried out and it remained in a state of disrepair until the early 19th century when the Smiths took up what must have been quite a challenge and employed the architect John Dobson to convert the ruin into a substantial mansion and fashionable country house with laid out parkland.

In 1862 the Crawshaw family came into possession, and added a west wing in 1876. In 1888 it was acquired by the Cruddas family. It served as a hospital during the Second World War, and is currently owned by the Braithwaite family. Charles Antony Elliot Braithwaite is a former barrister, businessman and politician.

The castle has its ghost story too, originating in the time when Sir John de Widderington was the Lord of Haughton Castle. He was known for being a good man who fought for peace during the lawless times in the borders. Sir John decided to go to York to visit Cardinal Wolsey who was there at the time. Before he left, his men caught a reiver rustling cattle in the local meadows. Sir John put the man in his dungeon at Haughton Castle, intending to deal with him when he returned from York.

On arrival in York after 2 days riding, Sir John realised he had the key of the dungeon in his pocket and he had forgotten to leave instructions with his staff to feed or water his prisoner, an omission that gave him great concern. So in haste he headed back to Haughton, but his horse dropped dead with exhaustion and by the time he reached the castle forty-eight hours later he was told that the prisoner had cried and moaned and screamed, but the noise had died down, and nothing had been heard since. When Sir John unlocked the cell he found the reiver dead.

The spirit of the prisoner haunted the castle, and night after night the sounds of his cries and moans could be heard around the countryside. It all kept Sir John and his staff awake at night, his servants left and the villagers demanded that he do something about it. So, Sir John called in the Rector of Simonburn to exorcise the ghost, after which nothing more was heard. As a comfort to Sir John, the Rector left him with the Bible from which he had read during the exorcism. However, when the Bible was sent to London for re-binding the reiver's moaning and screams returned to haunt the castle. Orders were given to return the Bible quickly from London and lay the spirit of the ghost to rest once again.

Local legend states that the screams from Haughton Castle can still be heard whenever a descendant of Sir John de Widderington sets foot inside the castle.

In spite of the various renovations and the 19th century Dobson rebuild, the house has retained its fine castellate appearance with slit windows, corner towers and crenellation. It is said to be one of the best-preserved hall houses in the north of England and is a popular film set location. A small number of cottages on the estate have been converted into holiday homes.

Stewardship/Management – privately owned/Braithwaite family

no dedicated website NE46 4AY

Resources and Further Reading

- www.barrasford.net/northumberland-attractions/haughton-castle.htm
- www.mjwayland.com/haunt-field/haughton-castle-ghost-story/

TWENTY SIX

LANGLEY CASTLE

Langley Castle is a Grade 1 listed, 14th century castle now operating as a highly sophisticated luxury hotel and events venue off the A686, 2 miles south of Haydon Bridge and 5 miles west of Hexham.

Set in magnificent countryside in the valley of the South Tyne, the hotel holds a raft of quality awards for accommodation, dining and wedding hosting. This truly is a castle in the traditional sense with a fairytale aspect of towers, crenellation, massive stone walls and internal rooms of great height and proportion. Huge fireplaces with blazing log fires, seats recessed into 7 feet-thick walls and stained-glass tracery windows create an atmosphere of baronial opulence. Those walls are said to have been built using material from Hadrian's Wall about 5 miles to the north. So historically fantastical is the ambiance of the castle that the author JK Rowling came to stay to gain inspiration for her one of her books – famous for the portrayal of the stereotypical medieval castle environment.

Courtesy Langley Castle

A remarkable feature of the building is the south-west tower, which has no fewer than 12 garderobes – the long-drop toilet. Conveniently, more modern facilities are available to the visitor today. The castle proprietors are passionate about its heritage and offer tours around the castle, the wider surrounding countryside, and the Roman forts at nearby Chesters, Vindolanda and Corbridge.

The site was originally the seat of the Barons of Tynedale in the 12th century. The castle itself was built in 1350 during the reign of Edward III by Sir

Thomas de Lucy, Baron of Langdale. Like many at that time Sir Thomas needed a strong tower house to secure himself against the belligerent activities of the Scots.

The castle then passed through marriage to Gilbert de Umfraville, Earl of Angus, and in 1381 following Gilbert's death to Henry de Percy, Earl of Northumberland. Henry IV sought to curb the power of the Percy family and in 1405 he attacked and burned the castle. He caused irreparable damage and thereafter the castle lay ruined for centuries, gathering ivy and decay.

In its ruined condition and together with its estate, it passed through the hands of various aristocratic families – the Dukes of Bedford, the Earls of Northumberland, Sir Reynold Carnaby and in the 17th century to the Earls of Derwentwater. James, the third Earl together with his brother Charles, took part in the failed Jacobite rising of 1715. For their involvement in this revolt against the English Crown they were executed by beheading at the Tower of London. A stone cross stands by the road from the castle to Haydon Bridge commemorating their loyalty to the King of Scotland.

Courtesy Langley Castle

The demise of the Earls of Derwentwater was an important event in the history of the castle because it was then confiscated by the Crown and taken out of private hands. Its administration passed to the Royal Naval Hospital at Greenwich, and signs of the Admiralty's influence can still be seen in the area - for example the anchor motif on the front of a house at Langley and the naming of a pub in Haydon Bridge, The Anchor.

However, the property remained a ruin until it was bought and restored by a local historian, Cadwallader Bates, Sheriff of Northumberland, in 1882. The restoration of the castle to its original 14th Century condition and specification became a life's work, not only for Cadwallader but also for his wife Josephine, who continued his work after Cadwallader's death in 1902. Josephine rebuilt the original chapel on the castle roof in memory of her husband and worked tirelessly until her own death in 1933. She is buried alongside her husband in the castle grounds.

The building then remained empty until it was used as a barracks in the Second World War, then in the post-war years as a girls' school. In the 1980s, it was bought by the Robb family, and then in 1986 it was acquired by Dr Stuart Madnick, a professor at the Massachusetts Institute of Technology who had acquired the Barony of Langley in 2007. Dr Madnick converted the property into the luxurious, prestige hotel it has become

Photos courtesy Langley Castle

Not to be outdone, the castle is another that has a ghost story. Castle staff and visitors claim to have seen an apparition, a crying woman who appears at a window before jumping to her death. She is reputed to be Maud de Lucy, widow of the Sir Thomas de Lucy who built the castle back in 1530. She was so broken-hearted upon receiving news of her husband's death at the Battle of Shrewsbury that she threw herself out of the window from which she had been waiting and watching for his return. An extreme demonstration of grief, no doubt. However, the story has been passed down through time and the identity of the ghostly lady seems to have become a little confused. It may have been Maud, or it may not. It doesn't really matter – a ghost is a ghost and if you're keen to have the living daylights frightened out of you then one suicidal spectre jumping out of a high window is probably as good as any.

This is a stunningly impressive venue, in one of the most beautiful parts of the Northumberland countryside, making it perhaps the most prestigious, historic castle hotels in the country.

Stewardship/Management –Privately owned/Dr Stuart Madnik/Langley Castle

www.langleycastle.co.uk NE47 5LU

As a hotel Langley Castle is open to the public, and provides the services and facilities one would expect of such a venue

Site-specific further reading:

- The Romance of Northumberland (Classic Reprint); A. G. Bradley; 2018 (original published 1909)
- news.mit.edu/2007/mits-very-own-baron [*Dr Stuart Mednik's association with Langley and the Barony*]

TWENTY SEVEN

LINDISFARNE (HOLY ISLAND) CASTLE

Lindisfarne, or Holy Island, is a tidal island off the north east coast of Northumberland, about 5 miles north of Bamburgh and 8 miles south of Berwick. It is approached from the main A1 road through the village of Beal to the modern, vehicular causeway or the ancient pilgrims' path marked with poles across the sand and mud flats. As the island is tidal the causeway is flooded and impassable when the tide is in. In spite of high-profile warnings on websites and on notice boards posted on the causeway itself, a number of people are caught out every year, requiring rescue by the coastguard or lifeboat services. This is usually accompanied by a deeply troubled frown from their motor insurers. For those who ignore the tide tables a stilted refuge hut can provide some temporary sanctuary.

Beyond the tidal section the road wanders past high dunes, skirting the bay, to approach the island village where an off-road, pay and display car park is as far as the casual visitor is supposed to take a vehicle. A few minutes' walk leads into the village itself with its shops, pubs, information centres and not least the exceptional Lindisfarne Mead brewery, distillery and outlet. From there, walking on along the coastal path beyond the church and the ruined priory, the castle rises high on the rocky mound known as "*Beblowe*".

Simon Hawkins

For good reason it's one of the most photographed castles in England. It rises majestically from the high outcrop of basalt as if it was a natural, organic part of the rock, but though it looks like a medieval fortress, looks can be deceiving as the castle is actually a 20th-century restoration of a Tudor fort.

The monastic history of Holy Island goes back to the 7th century when St Aiden, summoned from the Scottish island of Iona by King Oswald to spread the Word, established a monastery in about 634. The island became an important centre of Celtic Christianity under Saints Aidan, Cuthbert and Bede. However the castle itself came much, much later. 500 years before the monks were the Romans, but apart from the area around the Tyne valley and Hadrian's Wall the Romans did not much settle in the north east. It was somewhat uncivilised and barbaric for their tastes and remained pretty much unaffected by the occupation, especially in places as remote as Lindisfarne. Before the Romans there wasn't much at all, so the real history of Lindisfarne and hence its castle begins with those monks, and then the dastardly Vikings.

The island is cut off from the mainland twice a day, and a stilted refuge hut provides sanctuary for those who ignore the tides.

Photo by Nathan Atkinson

The monastery was vulnerable to incursions from across the North Sea by Viking raiders from the late 8th century to the time of the Norman invasion in 1066. The Vikings' violent and destructive behaviour led the monks of Lindisfarne to flee, taking the shrine of St Cuthbert with them, first to Chester-le-Street then finally to Durham Cathedral. After the Norman Conquest of 1066, and the Viking threat had receded, a Priory was established in place of the old monastery, home to the Benedictine order.

For many years the Priory bravely resisted the next threat, which came from the Scots, by fortifying the Priory buildings and maintaining a defensive presence throughout the 14th century. It was not until Henry VIII, piqued at the Catholic refusal to grant him a divorce, came along in 1536 with his English Reformation and put an end to the religious presence at Lindisfarne, physically if not spiritually.

Lindisfarne Priory was ruined and abandoned as a result of Henry's Dissolution, but the King ordered a fort to be built on the high mound to the north of the monastic ruins, overlooking the harbour. There may have been a small lookout tower on the site before Henry decided to build there, but little else at that time. The location is perfect for controlling access to the harbour.

In 1542 Henry VIII ordered Thomas Manners, 1st Earl of Rutland to fortify the site against possible Scottish invasion, and by December 1547 heavy guns had been installed. By 1549 the fort was completed. It is small by most standards, constrained as it was by the physical properties of the mound and the geography of the island. At first it was little more than an earthen bulwark, but during the Elizabethan period from 1558 further improvements and reinforcements were made. Proper defences were built in stone, using material from the priory ruins. Provision was made for gun batteries incorporating new developments in artillery technology, meaning heavier cannon, explosives and fire-power. Cannon probed through the battlements facing west – a warning to anyone who might approach with less than friendly intentions.

When James I came to power in England and combined the Scottish and English thrones by the Union of Crowns[5] in 1603 the need for a castle declined – a common story heard constantly in the history of medieval fortifications in the north east border lands. However, the castle remained garrisoned from Berwick and protected the small Lindisfarne harbour.

In the middle of the 17th century the English Civil War[2] troubled the island of Lindisfarne only slightly. It was blockaded by Royalists, but nothing came of it. Similarly, during the Jacobite Rising of 1715 there were half-hearted attacks, but it was quickly recaptured by soldiers from Berwick who imprisoned the rebels. It is said that the prisoners dug their way out and hid for nine days close to nearby Bamburgh Castle to make their escape.

Ken Lussey

Then the castle just sat there for many years. In Victorian times it attracted tourists and artists, but the castle itself received little attention. Then in 1902 Edward Hudson, publishing magnate and founder of Country Life magazine, discovered the castle apparently by chance, and he resolved to restore it and turn it into a place to which he could retreat from the pressures of city life – a sort of holiday home. He commissioned the architect Edwin 'Ned' Lutyens and garden designer Gertrude Jekyll to refurbish the castle and its grounds. Lutyens was instructed to adapt the garrison quarters into a house, and the Tudor cellars into a suite of living rooms.

The result is highly idiosyncratic. The dramatic entrance involves a steep climb around the rocky base, and inside the entrance hall is dominated by stone pillars and bare stone floors. Throughout, Lutyens used stone, brick, slate and wood to create his forms and textures, replicating the atmosphere of many years gone by.

Today there is much to explore. The remnants of the old Tudor fort are much in evidence, and one can explore the vaults, the ship room and the gun battery. The wide chimney-piece contains an old bread-oven, and Lutyens has incorporated Neo-Gothic traceried windows framed by curtains and contrasting colours in the walls and brick floors.

There are bedrooms to be investigated, the grand, long gallery, the music room and the use of exposed stone arches and oak beams that provide a feeling of the old Tudor and Elizabethan heritage. From the upper battery there are spectacular views of the wide and wild coastline and Northumberland's huge skies.

Photos Ken Lyons

Many of the features installed by Lutyens look original but they are actually mock-Tudor designs to mimic the feel if not the reality of the 16th century building. So fireplaces, wood panelled rooms, latched doors, decorative brick flooring and moulded roof beams are all made to appear Tudor. Lutyens dressed small rooms with huge pieces of furniture, created oddly unnecessary winding passages, added steps down followed by steps up and made low doorways in rooms with high ceilings.

A short walk from the base of the rock on which the castle stands is a small walled garden designed by Gertrude Jekyll. This was originally a vegetable garden for the fort's garrison, but Jekyll transformed it into a flower garden, which has now been fully restored by the National Trust using Jekyll's original plans and planting scheme.

The upturned boats of Lindisfarne are a noted feature of the island's culture and heritage. Lutyens used them as sheds and in spite of arson attacks and natural decay, they have either been replaced or renovated by the National Trust and now feature as a tourist attraction and subjects for photographers and artists.

And Lindisfarne has to have its ghost story too, according to the islanders. It is said that the ghost of St. Cuthbert haunts the ruins of the priory and the area around the castle. His spirit is seen mainly on nights when the moon is full and the tide is high across the roadway to the mainland. Or, one might wonder, just after the pubs have closed? The ghost of a phantom white dog also roams the ruins, so it is said.

Features nearby the castle include the 19th-century industrial lime kilns, the ruins of the old Priory, the present church, shoreline walks and the village facilities. The castle, garden and nearby lime kilns have been in the care of the National Trust since 1944 and are open to visitors. The view from the castle stretches south with the magnificent panorama of Budle Bay and Bamburgh Castle. To the north, the sweeping sands of Goswick, Cheswick, and Cocklawburn lead to Spittal, the river Tweed, the great walls of Berwick and on to the border with Scotland.

The castle at Lindisfarne is unique, a glimpse into a fascinating past and a visit to the coast of Northumberland is not complete without including it. Just don't miss the tide!

Stewardship/Management – National Trust

www.nationaltrust.org.uk/visit/north-east/lindisfarne-castle TD15 2SH

Guidebook – available on site or from National Trust

Admission: Charges apply; **Parking**: Paid car park off the road into the village; **Opening Times**: Seasonal, scheduled opening times for the castle, unlimited to the grounds; **Toilets**; **Café/Restaurants**; **Gift Shops**; **Exhibitions/Displays**; **On-site Management**; **Dogs** in grounds only; **Disabilities:** Access to the castle is steep and unsuitable for people with mobility issues

Site-specific further reading:

- www.lindisfarne.org.uk/
- www.islandshirearchives.org.uk/ [*extensive information about the island of Lindisfarne, its history and development*]

TWENTY EIGHT

MITFORD CASTLE

The ruins of Mitford Castle lie in the hamlet of Mitford just off the main A1 road 1 mile west of Morpeth, accessed locally by the B6343. It is a Scheduled Ancient Monument and a Grade I listed building. The Norman motte and bailey structure stands on a small prominence above the River Wansbeck and public access is freely available.

The names most associated with the castle are those of Mitford, Bertram and Middleton, all of whom by allegiance, subterfuge or Royal favour were in and out of possession of Mitford Castle over several centuries.

At the time of the Norman conquest in 1066 the castle, then simply an earthwork structure, was held by Sir John de Mitford. His only daughter, Sybilla, married one of William the Conqueror's Norman knights, Richard Bertram, and the property passed into the Bertram family. In 1138 it was described as the "*oppidum*" (*a chiefly walled or fortified settlement*) of William Bertram in 1138.

Fred Vincent

In time the property devolved to Roger Bertram. Roger was in opposition to King John who had held the throne of England since 1199, as were many of his Northern counterparts who supported Alexander II of Scotland. In 1215 the castle was seized from the rebellious Roger by King John, who gave it to his supporter Hugh de Balliol. It was garrisoned by the nobleman Philip de Ulecotes who withstood a siege by the Scots king Alexander. Following the death of King John in 1216, and that of Philip in 1220, the Regent for the underage heir to the English throne Henry III, William Marshall 1st Earl of Pembroke attempted to settle matters by reconciliation and ordered Mitford returned to the Bertram family. Thus, Roger Bertram returned to his home.

In 1264 the castle was seized from the Bertrams and given to William de Valence, King Henry's half-brother. In about 1270 Agnes Bertram transferred the castle to Eleanor, widow of King Henry III. She in turn granted it to her kinswoman Eleanor de Geneva. Through marriage to Eleanor in 1275, Alexander de Balliol, brother of John de Balliol became the new Lord of the castle.

Simon Hawkins

In 1292 Alexander's brother John de Balliol, was crowned King of Scotland following King Edward I's decision to reject all other claims to the throne, including Balliol's rivals, the Bruces.

Fred Vincent

The First War of Scottish Independence broke out in 1296. When Edward I died at the Battle of Bannockburn in 1314, Robert the Bruce began causing trouble in his attempts to force Edward II to recognise Scotland as an independent country. Sir Gilbert Middleton, a belligerent and forceful knight who had seized Mitford Castle from the Valence family sometime around 1310, took advantage of the disorder caused by the war and took the opportunity to further his own interests. He used the castle for kidnappings and as a gaol for high-profile prisoners captured from his rebellious raids across Northumberland and the Scottish Borders. On 1st September, 1317, he kidnapped Lewis de

Beaumont, Bishop of Durham, his brother Harry de Beaumont, two Italian cardinals and John de Felton, constable of Alnwick Castle. Sir Gilbert hoped to use de Felton to his advantage as a hostage in his ambition to obtain a grant to the prestigious Alnwick Castle. However, John de Felton's men were having none of it and made a surprise attack on Mitford, capturing both Gilbert and his brother John, who were both promptly taken to the Tower of London and executed by being hung, drawn and quartered.

In 1326 Mitford Castle was described as "*the site of a castle wholly burned*". It's unclear exactly how that came about. Perhaps it suffered a fire during Middleton's rebellious activities, or perhaps it was over-run by the Scots in 1318 during Middleton's imprisonment in the Tower of London awaiting his brutal execution.

The site of the ruins passed through marriage to the powerful Percys of Alnwick Castle, and then in the 1430s through marriage to Sir Thomas Burgh. In 1556 the castle and manor were sold back to the Mitford family, thereby returning it, as it were, to the hands that nurtured its beginnings 500 years before. In its burnt and decayed state the castle languished as part of the Mitford family estate until 1993, when it was bought from them by the Bruce Shepherd family. With the property at risk of further decay English Heritage have managed plans and grants to help towards the repair and restoration.

And does Mitford Castle have its ghost story? Of course it does. The tale is of a lord of the castle, precisely who and when is unclear, but perhaps a Mitford, a Bertram or a dastardly Middleton. In any case, it was in ancient times. The Lord was a drunkard and given to taking liberties with maidens in his charge. One such unfortunate girl was Rosie Armitage, a house maid. His Lordship imposed himself upon her and left her carrying his child. Unable to bear the shame Rosie hanged herself from an oak tree in the castle grounds. The tree is still there, known as '*Poor Rosie'* to this day. Poor Rosie's anguished soul may be seen through the damp half-light on a foggy winter's evening, usually just after the pubs have shut.

Given its dramatic history it's a shame so little of Mitford Castle survives today, However, the surviving stones occupy a pleasant, grassy, sheepy place to wander around, rest or take a picnic. It's easily accessible by a short stroll out of the village, from where the ruins can be seen high on their little hill.

Stewardship/Management – Shepherd family/English Heritage

No dedicated website

NE61 3PZ

Admission: Free; **Parking**: Free roadside; **Opening Times**; unlimited

There are no visitor services available at the site or in the small hamlet of Mitford

TWENTY NINE

MORPETH CASTLE

Morpeth Castle is a Scheduled Ancient Monument and a Grade I listed building. In terms of surviving structure there now remains only the gatehouse, restored by the Landmark Trust* and available to rent as a holiday home.

Set amidst the gardens and walks of Carlisle Park, the grounds and the "*Ha Hill*" on which the original structure once stood are freely accessible to the public. The park includes formal gardens, an aviary, play areas, a paddling pool, ancient woodland, picnic areas, toilets, tennis courts, bowling greens, a skate park and more. The site is within the town of Morpeth itself, and the usual pay and display parking arrangements generally apply nearby. The gatehouse can be viewed externally but inside access is for only those booked as residents.

The original motte and bailey dates from the 11th century and was built on a hill overlooking the river Wansbeck by the de Merlay family. Baron William de Merlay, of Norman heritage of course, built his castle and established his dynasty in about 1085. Referred to as the first castle of Morpeth, nothing remains of that original structure.

Derek Taylor

On June 15, 1215 the Magna Carta was signed at Runnymede by King John. Amongst many things it reduced the monarch's powers, but in the north the Northumberland barons were not happy about that and the potential reduction of their authority, and they transferred their allegiance from John to Alexander of Scotland. There followed conflict and raids into the south as far as Newcastle. In retaliation John attacked north to suppress the barons and in 1216 the castle at Morpeth was captured, burnt to destruction and the estates confiscated.

In 1271 the remains of what had been the first Morpeth castle passed from its original owners, the de Merlays, to the Greystoke family and the building now known as Morpeth Castle – so in fact the second castle - was built. It comprised a stone keep in the centre of a courtyard or bailey, protected by a curtain wall. An imposing gatehouse was added in the 1340s. Little of all that survives today apart from small sections of the curtain wall and the gatehouse, much-altered since Greystoke's original.

Simon Hawkins

The gatehouse lacks any significant defensive features, suggesting that the building was intended mainly for prestige rather than military strength. The Greystokes had other property in the area and Morpeth seems to have been intended as a centre of administration for local government and law. It was rarely visited by Greystoke himself, remaining under the control of a Constable who lived there with his household and a small garrison. No doubt there was also a Steward or Bailiff, and a clerk to oversee the management of Lord Greystoke's property in the area.

In 1516 Margaret Tudor, sister of Henry VIII and widow of James IV of Scotland, stayed for four months in Morpeth Castle as she fled from her enemies in Scotland. She was one of many Royal visitors to Morpeth over the centuries, an indication that that the castle was, in its day, both prestigious and relatively safe. For example, border raids were a common hazard but there is no record of the castle having been involved in serious fighting until 1644 during the English Civil War. Then, and in spite of its meagre defensive capabilities, a garrison of 500 held the castle for 20 days against Royalist forces of 2,700. Apparently, they surrendered with a somewhat arrogant "*whatever?*" A tradition perhaps maintained at St James' Park to this day?

From the illustrious families of de Merlay and Greystoke, the castle passed to the Dacres and ultimately to the Howards, the Earls of Carlisle. No one resided there for any length of time and for the next 200 years the castle was largely abandoned and pillaged for building stone. The gatehouse, however, was lived in, and underwent various re-modellings over the years. Nevertheless, early 19th-century engravings show it as dilapidated. Then, in about 1860, the

Earl of Carlisle repaired the gatehouse, the only surviving part of the old castle, as a home for his agent.

While hardly in the best of condition, in 1946 it was bought by the local Council and for a while became a somewhat bizarre council house. It's unlikely that its former, baronial owners would have been terribly impressed. By the 1980s, expensive repairs were needed, and the castle fell vacant, quickly becoming derelict.

In 1988 a lease was taken by the Landmark Trust which undertook a full refurbishment, restoring many of the gatehouse's original historic features and removing the modern additions - including a swimming pool. The gatehouse is now available to rent from the Landmark Trust as quality holiday accommodation.

The surrounding grounds and Carlisle Park provide an impressive location for walks and leisure, together with the most agreeable town and its facilities. A grand day out, perhaps.

* The Landmark Trust is a British building conservation charity, founded in 1965 by Sir John and Lady Smith, that rescues buildings of historic interest or architectural merit and then makes them available for holiday rental. Those who rent Landmarks provide a source of funds to support restoration costs and building maintenance

Stewardship/Management – Landmark Trust/Morpeth Town Council

www.landmarktrust.org.uk/search-and-book/properties/morpeth-castle-9482/#Overview [*recommended, informative website about the history and restoration of the castle*]

NE61 2PP

Situated in the town of Morpeth itself, all usual facilities including parking, toilets, shops and refreshments can be found locally. The area around the castle and Carlisle Park is dog-friendly and mostly suitable for people with disabilities.

THIRTY

NEWCASTLE

The boundaries of what we call "Northumberland" today have wandered about all over the place for centuries. It's been complicated, at times stretching from the Humber as far north as the Forth in present day Scotland. As a Kingdom it didn't really exist before about the 7th century, then becoming an amalgamation of older Anglo-Saxon provinces such as Deira and Bernicia, although purists and academics would say that is a gross simplification.

After the Romans left Britain in 410 and the Anglo-Saxon period began, what we now know as Newcastle became part of the powerful kingdom of Northumbria, and was known as Munucceaster (modernised as Monkchester) until 1400, when it became a county in its own right, separate from Northumberland. Since 1974, the city has been a part of the Metropolitan County of Tyne and Wear. However, since one can say that the castle at Newcastle has its origins as far back as Anglo-Saxon times, and on any view shortly after the Norman invasion of 1066, it seems reasonable to include it in a list of Northumberland castles.

The castle is situated in the heart of the city, overlooked by the railway lines that cross the river by way of the High Level Bridge. Closely surrounded by Georgian and Victorian buildings and the cathedral of St Nicholas, it has a stunning panorama over the city and the river quaysides. This medieval fortification was built on the site of the Norman fortress that gave the City of Newcastle its name. It's made up of two parts - the Castle Keep and the fortified gatehouse known as the Black Gate. The Keep is a Grade I listed building, and a Scheduled Ancient Monument. Both the Keep and the Gatehouse are owned by Newcastle City Council and managed by a charity, the Heart of the City Partnership. Public access is available to both the Keep and the Gatehouse - the only surviving parts of the castle along with some notable sections of the town walls and associated towers.

The Black Gate and the castle keep after dissection by the main railway line in 1849. The photograph is early 20th century

It all started in the 2nd century when the Roman occupiers built the first bridge across the Tyne and a fort to protect it. The course of Hadrian's Wall runs close by. The site was then known as Pons Aelius – the Bridge of Aelius - Aelius being the family name of Hadrian, responsible for the eponymous wall. It was pretty much the edge of the Roman world, and although there wasn't much here then it was a frontier the Romans were keen to establish and protect. Newcastle, as it was to become known, was little more than a military fort set beside the river protecting the bridge.

After the Romans' withdrawal in 410 the site came to be known by that name Monkchester, which suggests that there was a monastery here, but still little more. There was no sign of a great city at that time. In the late 7th century, a cemetery was established on the site of the old Roman fort and an Anglo-Saxon church was built.

In 1080 the new Norman king, William I, the Conqueror, sent his eldest son, Robert Curthose, north to defend the kingdom against the Scots. Robert went to Monkchester and began the building of a 'New Castle', giving the place the name by which we know it today. This was a motte-and-bailey affair, a wooden tower on top of an earthen mound (the motte), surrounded by a moat and wooden stockade (the bailey).

In 1095, Robert de Mowbray, Earl of Northumbria, rose up to challenge King William II - the third son of William the Conqueror and commonly known as William Rufus – from the Latin "*rufus*" meaning "*the red*" suggesting that William had red hair. Rufus sent an army north to crush Mowbray's revolt and to capture the castle, which he did. From then the castle became Crown property and an important stronghold from which the king could control the northern barons.

Not a trace of the Norman tower or the motte and bailey remain now, or of any of the wooden structure which Henry II replaced with stone in 1168. Most of the stonework we see in the present keep dates from this period – nearly 900 years old. The great outer gateway to the castle, called 'the Black Gate', was built later, between 1247 and 1250, in the reign of Henry III. It consisted of two towers with a passage running between them and a vaulted guardroom. There was a drawbridge at the front and another at the rear and a portcullis which could be raised and lowered to seal the entrance passage.

This new castle became an important stronghold in the northern defences against the Scots and a medieval town grew up around it. Its military importance and riverside location stimulated trade and commerce and the expanding town developed into a major port. By 1300 Newcastle's importance was such that it was permitted to appoint its own mayor and a century later the town became a county in its own right. "*The County of Newcastle*" is an unfamiliar and perhaps surprising title today, but that's what it was in 1400, independent of Northumberland and a law unto itself. Some might say that nothing much has changed.

In 1618 James I leased the gatehouse to a courtier, Alexander Stephenson, who substantially altered it, rebuilding the upper floors. Stephenson then let the Black Gate out to various tenants, one of whom was a merchant called Patrick Black. It was he who gave his name to the Black

Gate, which is disappointing in a way. "*Black Gate*" suggests something dark, nefarious and thoroughly unsavoury whereas it was, in fact, just some fellow's name.

In the 13th century stone walls with towers were constructed to enclose the town and provide additional protection. So effective were these walls in safeguarding the town that the defensive role of the castle itself was much diminished and this led to its neglect. Robert Maudit, the Sheriff in 1334, advised Edward III that since Bannockburn (1314) the castle buildings had deteriorated. Repairs were effected and in 1336 the sheriff was ordered to stop the townspeople from tipping rubbish into the castle ditch – fly-tipping is nothing new. It seems it didn't help much because in 1589 during the reign of Queen Elizabeth I the castle was described as being in ruinous condition. In 1618 houses were erected in the bailey and close by the walls. They were cramped, closely built, untidy buildings which did little to prevent the continuing degradation of the castle itself.

The Black Gate

In 1643, during the English Civil War[2], the Royalist Mayor of Newcastle, Sir John Marley, made various repairs to the Keep and refortified the castle. In 1644 the Scottish army crossed the border in support of the Parliamentarians and the Scottish troops besieged Newcastle for three months until the garrison surrendered. The encounter caused extensive damage to the town walls.

After that, from the early 17th century onward, the physical security of the castle was compromised by the construction of more shops and houses over much of the site. By 1800 there were a large number of dwellings and tenements within the boundaries of the castle and by the early part of the nineteenth century, the Black Gate had become a slum. Contemporary engravings depict all manner of depravity, from filth and poverty to gin-soaked prostitutes lolling about in the streets.

In response Newcastle Corporation bought the site in 1809 and demolished the slums. The Black Gate was leased to the Society of Antiquaries of Newcastle upon Tyne, which extensively restored it in the 1880s, adding the top floor and a pitched roof amongst other improvements. The drawbridges to the front and rear of the Black Gate were removed and replaced by wooden footbridges. The Society created a museum and held regular meetings there.

In the end it was the advent of the railway age that permanently changed the castle and left it much as we see it today. In 1849 the Victorian railway and the large viaduct, the High Level Bridge which carries the main line, was built through the castle site destroying much of the infrastructure and permanently separating the Gatehouse from the castle Keep. As a result, only the Keep and the Black Gate now remain.

The castle keep

Naturally, the castle is haunted, reputedly at least. There are numerous ghostly stories ranging from sounds and sights to unexplained mists and shadows. Cameras are said to have recorded hundreds of dark shadows, orbs, and mists. Visitors have felt the temperature drop without reason, and people have been touched by invisible hands. There have been reports of chanting in the Queen's chamber, echoing around the walls of the Keep. A mysterious, diaphanous lady has been seen in the chamber and in the chapel. Visitors have reported being attacked, scratched and shoved within the walls of Castle Keep.

The most famous ghost is called the "Poppy Girl". Legend has it that she is the ghost of a flower girl sent to prison because she owed money. While in prison, she was raped and beaten to death by the male prisoners. She is often seen on the stairs of the Keep and it is said that when she is nearby, a whiff of flowers is present in the air. Or a whiff of Newcastle Brown Ale, more likely.

The Castle at Newcastle is a reminder of the days of Royal Authority, when armies gathered and criminals were imprisoned and executed. It is a real, physical history lesson and is where the story of Newcastle began, and the reason the city got its name.

The Castle and the Keep open up the ancient city's heritage. The modern visitor will find much to explore - from a royal fortress to grim dungeons, ancient passageways and chambers. Exhibits allow visitors to experience what life would have been like for the inhabitants of these two astonishingly well-preserved medieval buildings.

Newcastle is a heavy old city, and its great stone architecture surrounds the site. The old walls can be explored, and the industrial heritage of the river Tyne is right on the doorstep. The history of the railway and the industries of shipbuilding and coal upon which the industrial heritage of the city is founded encloses the remains of this ancient fortress.

Medieval defences of Newcastle upon Tyne showing town wall and the castle

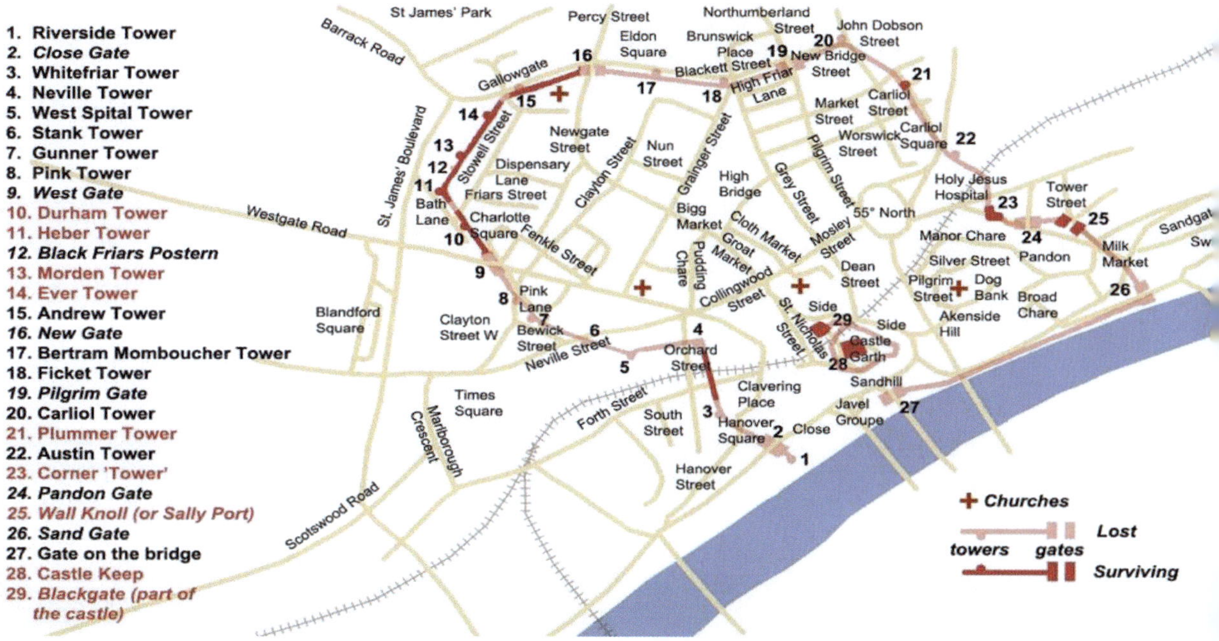

The site is currently owned by Newcastle City Council and managed by the Heart of the City Partnership charity. Both the Keep and the Gatehouse can be visited today, and the Castle also hosts weddings, learning events, various tours and experiences and offers itself as a venue for hire. From the battlements there are commanding views over the city and the river Tyne quayside, the cathedral and Newcastle station.

Stewardship/Management – Newcastle City Council/The Heart of the City Partnership

www.newcastlecastle.co.uk NE1 1RQ

There are a number of guide and reference books available. The official guidebook is available on-site or online

Admission: Charges apply; **Parking**: Limited on-street nearby; public pay car parks; **Opening Times**: Scheduled opening times; **Toilets**; **Café/Restaurant**; **Gift Shop**; **Exhibitions/Displays**;

Site-specific further reading:

- www.hauntedrooms.co.uk/castle-keep-newcastle
- 1stnorth.co.uk/the-black-gate

THIRTY ONE

NORHAM CASTLE

The ruined Norham Castle lies 5 miles south-west of Berwick, just outside the village of Norham overlooking the river Tweed and right on the England/Scotland border. It is a Grade I listed building and a Scheduled Ancient Monument, now in the care of English Heritage and open to visitors.

The castle stands on the south bank of the river Tweed, high above the river, so that the north side is protected by a steep slope. A deep ravine protects the east side and an artificial moat was dug round the west and south sides to complete the site's security. The castle had both an inner and outer ward, or partition, the inner on a mound separated from the outer by a moat crossed by a stone causeway and a drawbridge. This led to the strongly fortified West Gate, also known as "*Marmion's Gate*", the main entrance to the castle. There was an additional gate to the south known as the "*Sheep Gate*".

Aerial photos by Fred Vincent

The drawbridge has now been replaced by a wooden bridge. On the north side of the inner ward was the bishop's hall, 60 ft by 30 ft and now in substantial ruin. To the east side of the inner ward stands the keep, 84 ft by 60 ft, 88 feet high and in large part intact. Today, what's left of what was once a principal border castle is that great Keep and some surrounding ruined walls and low stonework.

Situated right on the border, the castle was constantly involved in the conflicts between English and Scots. It was in and out of the hands of one side or the other on so many occasions it's hard to keep count, but it's reckoned that the Scots besieged it nine times, and captured it on four. An account of the history of the castle is a ping-pong exchange of ownership, occupation and belligerent assertion.

So, sometimes in the hands of the Scots, sometimes with the English, the castle's principal incumbent for many centuries was the diocese, or bishopric, of Durham, meaning that it fell under the authority and administration of the Bishop of Durham, as did a good part of the lands around. In the medieval period the Bishops of Durham enjoyed enormous, almost unchallenged power in return for enforcing order along the English–Scottish border. The Prince Bishops, whose origins lie in the preceding centuries, ruled in the north east like Royalty. Antony Bek, steward to the Bishop of Durham in the late 13th century said, *"There are two Kings in England, namely the Lord King of England wearing a crown in sign of his regality, and the Lord Bishop of Durham wearing a mitre in place of a crown in sign of his regality in the Diocese of Durham."*

It was one of those Bishops of Durham, Ranulph Flambard, who founded the castle on the site of a much earlier prehistoric fort. The Bishop gave orders for its construction in 1121 in order to protect the property of the bishopric from incursions by the Scots. The fortress was rudimentary - little more than an earthen ringwork with a timber palisade around a ceremonial hall. It guarded a strategically important ford over the river Tweed, the road into, and from, Scotland. Norham was part of a defensive string of castles guarding the Tweed crossings between England and Scotland, along with the castles at Wark and Berwick.

Simon Hawkins

It didn't take long for the Scots to take offence at the new castle, and in 1136 David I of Scotland attacked and captured it. Political argy-bargy resulted in it being handed back to the bishopric, but the Scots were determined and captured it again in 1138. The structure was substantially damaged during all this, remaining derelict until Hugh de Puiset, Bishop of Durham from 1153 to 1195, had it all rebuilt. That de Puiset's rebuild was done at the command of Henry II speaks of Norham's importance. The rebuild was done on a grand scale, with a great tower on the site of Flambard's original two-storey hall.

In 1174 the good Bishop, unwisely as it turned out, supported the Scottish rebels in a revolt against Henry II when the Scottish king, William the Lion, invaded Northumberland. However, the rebels were defeated and, with some justification, King Henry doubted Bishop de Puiset's loyalty and kicked him out, taking possession of the castle. He put in a Crown Constable and garrisoned it with Royal soldiers. This continued until 1197, two years after Hugh's de Poiset's death, when it was restored to his successor, the more favoured Philip of Poitou, loyal to the King of England. When Philip died in 1208 the castle reverted to Royal control, after which King John maintained the defences in good order and provided a strong garrison. The defences proved themselves in 1215 when Alexander II of Scotland, son of William the Lion, besieged the castle for forty days but was successfully resisted. In 1217 the castle was once again restored to the bishopric of Durham.

Ken Lussey

Norham played its part in an important historic event in May 1291 when the Bishop of Durham, Anthony Beck, hosted Edward I at the castle while the king arbitrated between the 13 competitors for the Scottish throne (a process known as the Great Cause). John Baliol was the favoured contender and pronounced King of Scotland in 1292. Three days later Baliol paid his feudal homage to Edward in the hall at Norham.

Their accord was short-lived. In 1296 Edward invaded Scotland, and during the campaign his Queen, Marguerite of France, was accommodated at Norham Castle. This was actually rather too close to the border for comfort, but an indication of the trust the King had in the castle's security.

During the early fourteenth century, the Scots invaded Northumberland several times. In 1318 Robert the Bruce besieged the castle for nearly a year. His army succeeded in occupying the outer ward for three days but were driven out and the siege failed. Undeterred, the Scots returned in 1319 and the castle successfully withstood another siege of seven months. No lessons having been learned, in 1322 there was yet another attempted, unsuccessful Scottish siege.

In 1327 a Scottish army did manage to capture Norham, but it was soon restored to the Bishopric again and peace was, for a time, restored.

Throughout the fifteenth century the castle's defences were kept in good repair, a condition which served it well during the Wars of the Roses[3]. In 1462 Norham Castle was held by the Yorkists on behalf of Edward IV, and during this time sieges by the Lancastrians were successfully resisted. A great deal depended, including one's own survival, on being on the winning side and, betting unwisely in 1464, the Yorkists holding Norham castle changed sides to support the Lancastrians. They were forced to surrender without a fight after the Yorkist victory at Hexham. Both victorious Yorkist kings, Edward IV and later his brother Richard III, were careful to see the castle was properly maintained, garrisoned and provisioned. This demonstrates how vital they considered it to the security of the border with Scotland.

The Scots had another try in 1497 and besieged the castle for two weeks with an army led by James IV. The siege included the use of artillery to try to breach the walls but the garrison was finally relieved by an English army and the siege repelled. Following this latest attack the castle survived in English hands and was repaired again.

The terrifying cannon "Mons Meg" had unheard of firepower and caused massive damage to the castle

Undeterred, and with commendable persistence, King James IV of Scotland returned and invaded again, in 1513, laying siege to the castle whilst King Henry VIII was away campaigning in France. This time the Scots brought big guns with them. The huge artillery included a massive cannon known as "*Mons Meg*" - a devastating 20 inch diameter barrel which fired stone balls weighing a crushing 386 lb each. Mons Meg had been made in France and given to the Scottish King James II by the Duke of Burgundy as a sign of his support for the Scottish cause, and it was a frighteningly powerful weapon. The Scots guns pounded the castle's outer defences until, after two days of heavy bombardment, the walls fell to bits and the Scots stormed in. The garrison, out-numbered, out-gunned and out of ammunition, were forced to surrender. The bombardment resulted in massive damage to the castle and most of the outer walls were destroyed. Only weeks later, James was defeated and killed at the Battle of Flodden, and Norham fell into English hands again, restored to the Bishops of Durham.

Bishop Thomas Ruthall of Durham, the ruling bishop in Durham at the time, wanted to see for himself what had become of his property and travelled to Norham to view the wrecked castle. He found only the keep and west wall left standing and immediately set about putting it back together again. Thereafter the castle was maintained in a state of good repair, with a strong garrison during the remaining conflicts with Scotland in that century.

It didn't last long though as peace, of a sort at least, descended on the borders at the end of the 16th century. It is known that further repairs were carried out in 1554, but when this relative calm existed between the two countries the garrison was reduced and the redundant defences were allowed to deteriorate. The floors of the hall, parlour, and kitchen were perilously rotten and propped up with ship's masts. In 1596 Queen Elizabeth stated that she would spend nothing more on Norham, and with the union of the English and Scots crowns[5] in 1603 it fell into irrecoverable decay.

When James VI of Scotland acceded to the throne of England, he gave both the castle and the manor to George Home, 1st Earl of Dunbar, but it was never involved in further conflict or had any further defensive purpose and was left to fall into ruin.

One of J M W Turner's paintings of Norham castle (about 1822) Tate Britain (CCL)

In 1923 after passing through various hands the ruins were placed in the care of the state, and ultimately to the stewardship of English Heritage.

In the nineteenth century, the ruins of Norham Castle became well known from the paintings of J. M. W. Turner. He first painted the castle in 1797, but returned to paint it many times, finding inspiration in the romantic aspect of the old castle, capturing its atmosphere in ethereal pastel colours and vibrant sunsets. Several examples of his work can be seen in the Tate Gallery in London.

For the visitor today, the small town of Norham is a pleasant place where visitor services are available, including shops, a pub, buses, accommodation and walks down to the banks of the river Tweed. The castle site is but a few hundred yards from the town centre.

Stewardship/Management – English Heritage

www.english-heritage.org.uk/visit/places/norham-castle

TD15 2JY

Guidebook available from English Heritage and from local retail outlets

Admission: Free; **Parking**: Free; **Opening Times**: Scheduled opening times.; **Dogs** on leads only; **Disabilities:** The site is unlikely to be suitable for visitors with mobility issues

Site-specific further reading:

- Norham Castle; 2016 (reprint); Sir Hubert E. H. Jerningham
- www.flodden1513ecomuseum.org/places/local/norham-castle [*extensive information*]
- www.berwickfriends.org.uk/history/norham/

Ken Lussey

Fred Vincent

THIRTY TWO

ENGLISH HERITAGE

PRUDHOE CASTLE

The town of Prudhoe is on the south bank of the river Tyne, about 8 miles west of Newcastle city centre. Many years ago it would have been a country village at most and the castle, standing in an elevated position above the river, would have surveyed a landscape of rolling woodland. Then, as the industrial age developed, the structures of mining and heavy manufacturing arose and gradually Prudhoe succumbed to the encroachment of modern urbanity. Now, although the heavier and dirtier relics of the industrial revolution have long gone, it sits amongst light industry and housing estates, the road from Newcastle a more or less continuous ribbon of development. That said, the site itself is shielded from most of that, surprisingly quiet and secluded, an enclave of leafy serenity with an atmosphere of ancient times.

Ron Lyons

The route to the site, passing a mill-pond and heavy stone gatehouse, is enclosed by woodland and walks. Through the gatehouse are the ruins of the old castle, the 12th century keep and a later 19th-century house. Situated here in the outer bailey were the kitchens, bakehouse, brewhouse, and stables, as well as secondary lodging. Trails wander around the outside of the motte, through the grounds and ruins with views of the well-preserved outer walls.

The castle is a very substantial ruin. Its solidity clearly demonstrates the high-status position it once held and its honour as the only stronghold in Northumberland to defy the Scots, never taken by siege or assault. In its day it was a prestigious, comfortable and secure place for an aristocratic noble family to live. The old medieval ruins incorporate an early 19th century Georgian mansion, now in use within the castle walls as a visitor centre with exhibitions, a shop and other visitor facilities.

The Umfravilles and the Percys are the family names associated most with Prudhoe, The Umfravilles to begin with soon after the Norman conquest and then, as their line died away and stronger dynasties prevailed, the Percys.

The Umfravilles were granted the Barony of Prudhoe by William the Conqueror in the closing years of the 11th century following the Norman invasion of Britain. Back then, Newcastle was an insignificant site, and the open swathes of potentially lawless countryside needed policing for the security of the new Norman barons. The Umfravilles built the first castle at Pruhoe around 1100 to guard a ford across the Tyne, and not long afterwards Robert de Umfraville replaced the original wooden motte and bailey structure with a rampart of clay and stones, a stone curtain wall and a gatehouse.

Ken Lussey

Robert Umfraville died in 1145 at the age of 75 and his son, Odinell, become Baron of Prudhoe. Odinel rebuilt much of the castle and constructed the great Keep.

Umfraville took the side of Henry II of England in 1151, and King William the Lion of Scotland was unimpressed at this turn of allegiance away from the Scottish cause, so he attacked Prudhoe in 1173. He was beaten off but came back again in 1174, taking Harbottle Castle and laying siege to Prudhoe. Once again he was rebuffed, and William was captured after giving up the siege.

Odinel Umfraville died in 1182 and his son Richard succeeded to the Barony of Prudhoe. Allegiance was everything in those days, and getting it right was fundamental to one's standing in society, and indeed one's personal survival. Richard Umfraville didn't choose well and joined the barons standing against King John, who was not amused. Richard's stand against King John was not successful and in defeat he forfeited his estates to the Crown, although after King John died they were reinstated in 1217. Richard Umfraville died in 1226 and was succeeded first by his son, Gilbert, then by his grandson, also Gilbert. Through his mother, Gilbert II inherited the title of Earl of Angus, with vast estates in Scotland, but he continued to spend much of his time at Prudhoe.

Gilbert died in 1308 and was succeeded by his son, Robert D'Umfraville IV. In 1314, Robert was taken prisoner by the Scots at Bannockburn and deprived of the Earldom of Angus and of his Scottish estates, but he retained Prudhoe and after his release King Edward gave him the job of securing the castle and maintaining there a garrison of 40 men-at-arms and 80 horse.

When the last male heir of the Umfraville family died in 1381 after some 300 years of Umfraville rule at Prudhoe, his widow, Matilda, married Henry Percy, 1st Earl of Northumberland. On her death in 1398, the castle passed to the Percy family and thus the Percys ended the Umfraville rule and added to their already substantial estates. Taking over the barony of Prudhoe, they became the most powerful noble family in the north of England.

Ron Lyons

Percy is a name almost synonymous with Northumberland. They were the Earls, and later the Dukes, of Northumberland after all. However, The Percys - of whom there are a confusingly large number of Henrys – had a tendency towards misplaced allegiance. In spite of their power and influence they were in and out of favour, and the hangman's noose, on more occasions than you could shake a stick at. Their hold on Prudhoe – and on many of their other estates – came and went with one King or another and with their, sometimes unwise, political loyalties.

Henry Percy, 1st Earl of Northumberland, along with his son Henry "Hotspur" Percy, led a rebellion against the King. They fought against Henry IV and took part in the Battle of Shrewsbury. This went down badly with the King. When the rebellion was put down and the Crown's authority restored, Percy's punishment, as was the usual case for misdemeanors of that sort, was to be deprived of his estates. These, including Prudhoe, were forfeited to the Crown in 1405. There it remained, apart from a brief period in the keeping of the King's son the Duke of Bedford, for nearly 40 years. It was then the Percys resorted to the courts of law where they had powerful friends, and regained ownership of the Prudhoe estates in 1440. However, Henry Percy, 3rd Earl of Northumberland, was another who chose his friends badly and fought on the Lancastrian side in the Wars of the Roses[3]. He was killed at the Battle of Towton in 1461. Edward IV granted Prudhoe to his younger brother George, Duke of Clarence, but George also supported the wrong side and had only a brief tenure before the King exercised his Royal prerogative and gave the lot to Lord Montague, recently elevated to that status and an old adversary of the Percys.

Ron Lyons

The castle was restored to the fourth Earl of Northumberland, Henry Percy, in 1470. The principal seat of the Percys was Alnwick Castle and Prudhoe was for the most part let out to tenants. In the early 16th century however, another Henry Percy the 6th Earl lived there, as did his brother Sir Thomas Percy. Both the Earl and Sir Thomas were heavily involved in the Pilgrimage of Grace[10], a popular revolt against the Crown in 1536. Both were convicted of treason and executed. Following forfeiture of the estates (again) in August 1537 the castle was reported to have habitable houses and towers within its walls, although they were said to be somewhat decayed and in need of repairs.

When the Percys got it back again in about 1557 the castle was once again restored to Thomas Percy, the 7th Earl of Northumberland. But he got himself involved in the Rising of the North in 1569 for which he was convicted and executed in 1572.

The castle passed largely unscathed through the English Civil War[2], but by the late 17th century the Percy family had moved everything to Alnwick and left Prudhoe in the hands of the Earl's officials. It was rented out to local farmers and by 1776 it had ceased to have any real military function and was reported to be ruinous.

Ken Lussey

Between 1808 and 1817, Hugh Percy, 2nd Duke of Northumberland carried out substantial repairs to the ancient fabric. He demolished the old dwellings within the walls and built a rather grand Georgian mansion adjoining the keep and incorporating the medieval walls. It was clearly meant to be a residence for a gentleman, and was occupied by the Duke's land agent, William Laws. However, it did not survive for any habitable purpose and in 1966 the castle, by then mostly in ruin but with the intact Georgian mansion within its walls, was given over to the Crown. It is now managed by English Heritage and is open to the public. It is a Scheduled Ancient Monument and a Grade I listed building.

Ken Lussey

Prudhoe Castle is not unencumbered by the presence of the spooks and spirits of the past either. A white horse has been seen soundlessly pacing the outer ward. Chanting has been heard from the castle chapel. In the East Tower a ball has been heard bouncing up and down the stairs, yet no person nor ball has ever been observed during these occurrences. In the hall of the Georgian manor house, a cumbersome, heavy oak table top once fell to the floor during the night, apparently causing the whole house to shake.

And there's more. One night a couple who lived in the castle were in the room where the English Heritage shop is today. The husband was startled by sounds outside the window, and believing it to be an intruder he flung open the curtains to see a white shape rushing towards him. Was it the white horse of Prudhoe Castle, a more sinister spirit, or simply a trick of light? The fact that he suffered some sort of paralysis at the time suggests it may have had more to do with the wine he had at dinner rather than any sort of spiritual encounter. But who knows?

The site itself is remarkably leafy and shielded from the urban sprawl that surrounds it. Built by the Umfravilles and occupied, on and off at any rate, by the Percys, it's an exceptional place where every stone is a reminder of days long gone and a deep, fascinating history.

There are picnic areas within the castle walls, and English Heritage have provided displays explaining its long history, with hands-on exhibits to entertain visitors young and old. A Grand Day Out, one might say.

Stewardship/Management – English Heritage

www.english-heritage.org.uk/visit/places/prudhoe-castle

NE42 6NA

Admission: Charges apply; **Parking**: Free nearby; **Opening** Scheduled opening times; **Toilets**; **Café**; **Gift Shop**; **Exhibitions/Displays**; **On-site Management**; **Dogs** on leads; **Disabilities:** disabled access and facilities are reasonably well provided, with limited disabled parking

Resources and Further Reading

- www.prudhoelocalhistory.com/proud-heights-or-prudharsquos-hill.html [*the website of the Prudhoe Local History Society and probably the best online resource for the history of the castle and its environment. Highly recommended for those wishing to explore the castle in greater detail. Many excellent photos, including old, historic prints*]

THIRTY THREE

THIRLWALL CASTLE

The castle lies just outside the village of Greenhead, not far from the border with Scotland in the far west of the county. It's just off the A69, above the Tipalt Burn, a tributary of the river South Tyne. Located about 20 miles west of Hexham and 15 east of Carlisle, the site more or less straddles the routes of both Hadrian's Wall and the Pennine Way. Just a few hundred yards away is the renowned Roman Army Museum, operated by the Vindolanda Charitable Trust, with audio/visual displays, exhibits, 3D film and even holographics about all things Roman. Thirlwall Castle is a Grade I listed building and Scheduled Ancient Monument.

Simon Hawkins

The name Thirlwall is probably derived from "*a breach in the wall*", possibly referring to the Roman Wall. The castle is a ruin today, but in its time it was a prestigious family seat, a fortress and the principal home of the Thirlwall family. Its origins date to the period 1153-1165 when King Malcolm IV of Scotland created a barony here, and the first Baron of Thirlwall built a timber manor house.

In the 1330s one of the earlier Thirlwells, John, built an impressive stone fortress that would provide protection for the Thirlwall family for more than 400 years. The Castle itself is first recorded in 1369 and was built largely from stone taken from the old Hadrian's Wall. No licence to crenellate[4] appears to exist.

Designed for strength rather than home comfort, the fortress was unlikely to have been Thirlwall's main home, the manor house probably remaining the main residence.

The site chosen by John Thirlwall – a sheltered, wooded bank of the Tipalt Burn - was not naturally defensive, but it was surrounded by hill-top positions that provided vantage points for observation and security against potential intruders. All the materials he needed were close to hand, especially an abundant supply of dressed sandstone blocks which Hadrian and his army had quarried to build the Roman Wall more than 1000 years earlier. Thirlwall built the castle to last, to impress his guests, and as a deterrent to unwanted visitors.

Simon Hawkins (above) Fred Vincent (below)

The Thirlwalls had acquired wealth in Royal military service. They competed with other local families for land, status, influence and as vital security for their family, land and possessions. These family strongholds became important elements in the defence of the English border against Scottish attacks and combined they formed an effective chain of defence, guarding private estates as well as helping to defend national sovereignty.

The Thirlwell family continued to occupy the castle and the Barony of Thirlwell, some of them claiming their place in history in one way or another. Sir Percival Thirlwall was Richard III's standard-bearer during the Battle of Bosworth Field, the penultimate battle in the Wars of the Roses[3] on 22 August 1485. Fighting in the Yorkist cause alongside King Richard, Sir Percival, with consummate bravery, held the standard of his King aloft whilst fighting a desperate fight, continuing to do so even after his legs had been cut from under him. Even with the loss of his legs he is said to have held the standard until his last breath. Sadly for Sir Percival, his heroic stand was to no avail, as Richard was killed and the kingdom lost on Bosworth field.

Simon Hawkins

Anyway, back to Sir Percival's family seat at Thirwall Castle. In spite of its relative proximity to the border with Scotland, it was never attacked by either Scots or English and survived well until the English Civil War[2] of 1642 when it was commandeered by Scottish troops aiding the Parliamentarians. It seems they made such a mess of the place that it was not considered worth repairing. It is not recorded how a group of soldiers managed to do that to a building of such strength and solidity, but we've all been to parties that have got a bit out of hand, so perhaps that was it.

The last of the Thirlwall family line, Eleanor Thirlwall, abandoned the castle as a residence, and when she married Matthew Swinburne of Capheaton Hall in 1738 the estate passed to the Swinburne family. By the 1660s, the Thirlwalls had moved to Hexham, and in 1748 the

Swinburns sold the estate to the Earl of Carlisle. The Earl, being interested only in the land, allowed the Castle to fall into gradual decay. Nature and wildlife took over and the fabric of the castle began to crumble.

In 1831 the entire east wall of the castle fell into Tipalt Burn and there were serious collapses of masonry as the castle fell into irrecoverable decay. Stones were stolen from the castle walls to build nearby buildings. In 1999 the Northumberland National Park Authority took over the management of the castle to protect it from further dereliction. Under their management the site is open to the public with free, unlimited access.

In the 18th century, the crumbling ruins of Thirlwall Castle, its links with Hadrian's Wall and its melancholy, romantic appearance attracted artists and historians. Many came to paint and sketch the castle and the cottages that had sprung up within the shadow of its walls.

Naturally, legends abound. It is said, for example, that Baron John Thirlwell returned to the castle from foreign wars with treasure that included a solid gold table. It was so valuable that it came with its own guardian - a hideous dwarf with skin the colour of pitch. Hearing of this the Scots wanted the table for themselves and carried out many raids, all unsuccessful until they finally triumphed and went to claim their prize. They found the chamber empty with both table and dwarf nowhere to be found. One of the Scottish raiders claimed to have seen the dwarf hauling the table to the castle well where he threw it in, then jumping in after it before magically sealing the well. If you believe the legends, the dwarf is still down there, guarding his treasure in an underground cavern below the castle foundations.

Stewardship/Management – Northumberland National Park Authority

www.northumberlandnationalpark.org.uk/places-to-visit/hadrians-wall/thirlwall-castle

CA8 7HY

Guidebook/Leaflet available from Northumberland National Park's website

Admission: Free; **Parking**: Free/roadside; **Opening Times**: Unlimited.; **Toilets/Facilities** in nearby village; **Dogs; Disabilities:** No specific provision

THIRTY FOUR

TWIZELL (also TWIZEL) CASTLE

Only a few hundred yards from the England/Scotland border, the castle lies about 6 miles south-west of Berwick, off the A698 on the river Till, a tributary of the Tweed only half a mile away.

Rising above the medieval bridge that spans the Till, the land surrounding the ruined castle contains the earthwork remains of the lost medieval village of Twizel. The ruin itself, as it is now, presents the remains of an 18th-century castle which was never fully completed. It is a Grade II listed building and a Scheduled Ancient Monument currently in very poor condition and on the English Heritage At Risk Register. Although fenced off for safety and security reasons, it can be viewed from the public pathways very close by and, with some discretion, explored.

Simon Hawkins

Originally, there was a two-storey hall house here, probably built by the Redel family, lords of Tillmouth who purchased the Twizel estate in 1272. William Redel was constable of Norham and High Sherriff of Northumberland. By 1415 it was held by Sir John Heron who added a tower, a large internal kitchen fireplace, and fortified it all with a barmkin (a defensible enclosure).

The remarkable splendour of Twizell castle as it was towards the end of the 19th century, with the Twizell bridge (1511) in the foreground. It is hard to imagine the grandeur of the castle in the ruins that remain

Photo courtesy of Coldstream & District Local History Society.

In 1496 James IV invaded England and destroyed much in his path, including Twizell Castle. Although James and his army retreated promptly when by confronted by the English forces from Newcastle, the castle was left in a sorry state.

The nearby Twizel Bridge was built in 1511, providing the only dry crossing over the River Till between Etal and the Tweed. This bridge has historical significance as both the English and the Scottish army crossed here before engaging each other at the Battle of Flodden. When James IV passed on 24 August 1513 on his way to besiege Norham Castle, he held a council at Twizell, or "Twesil" or "Twesilhaugh"as it was then called. But even then the damage that had been caused by the Scots in 1496 was still unrepaired and the castle at Twizell was in poor shape.

The estate was sold by the Herons to the Selby family in about 1520. In 1561 it was still described as '*decayed and cast downe*', but John Selby set about repairing the buildings, creating a new chamber, a gallery, and chambers in the tower. Surviving documentation shows that it had battlements, pinion gables and a separate privy, more of a luxury back then than you might want to think about. Selby was a Gentleman Porter of Berwick-upon-Tweed and deputy to the border warden Lord Grey in the Berwick garrison, and by 1585 he was living regularly at Twizel. There is little of that medieval structure left now.

In 1685 Sir Francis Blake purchased the estate, and later in about 1770, a descendent, also called Sir Francis Blake, set about rebuilding the castle as a Gothic Revival mansion. He had great ambitions for it. It was to be five storeys high, a grand, sumptuous building of opulent proportions. He demolished the tower, clad the building with Gothic masonry and added turreted wings linked by a corridor giving separate access to the hall and chambers. The design, however, was badly flawed as the corridor was very low, narrow and difficult to weatherproof. The medieval stairs were inconvenient and the house was not really suitable for the needs of an 18th-century baronet. In any case he didn't fully finish it.

Moreover, the design was unpopular and ridiculed by contemporary commentators. It was effectively a folly on the site of what remained of the ruined castle. It was said that instead of the old tower there now stood "*an unseemly mass of unfinished masonry possessing not one single feature of castellated architecture*".

Simon Hawkins

The work went on for some forty years, but was never completed. The Blakes' family problems intervened and the ambitious project remained incomplete until the 1860s when it was inherited by Eleanor Stag Blake (the Stag and Blake families had inter-married). It was Eleanor's intention to complete the building before her eldest son Francis Douglas Blake came of age. This involved some major alterations – the first-floor entrance hall, already becoming outdated in 1800, had to be altered to provide a ground floor entrance. The result was a huge structure, a grand, sumptuous building of opulent proportions.

Unfortunately, although Mrs. Stag Blake spent a good deal of money, and her son's inheritance, on all that work, her son did not like the house and could not afford to run it. By the time he inherited it in 1880 his estates were losing money. Contemporary records show that he was selling houses, letting a farm, shutting his stables and moving his mother to a cottage on the estate. By 1881 he decided to demolish it and re-use the stone for his new mansion at Tillmouth Park just a few hundred yards away. Much of the incomplete Twizel Castle was demolished and the stone used in the new construction, but some of it was saved.

There was a developing public view at the time that historic buildings ought to be preserved and safeguarded against irrecoverable decay. Late in the late 19th century, following a newspaper campaign in the Berwick Advertiser, Blake agreed that the demolition would exclude those parts of the original, medieval castle that still existed. Thus, Eleanor Blake's great castle/mansion was lost, but what remains is the old, medieval structure. It may not be much, perhaps, of what was or might have been, but a reminder of a deep and fascinating history.

In many ways it is astonishing that the great mansion castle partially built by Eleanor Blake has been reduced to the ruin we see today. But the visitor will find detail in the crumbling stones that discloses the artistry, and indeed the opulence, of what was intended here.

Fred Vincent

Stewardship/Management – Privately owned

No specific website

TD12 4UX

Admission: Free; **Parking**: small off-road parking area within about 200 yards; **Opening Times**: Unlimited; **Dogs**; **Disabilities:** No specific provision

Site-specific further reading:

- www.berwickfriends.org.uk/history/twizel-castle/

THIRTY FIVE

TYNEMOUTH CASTLE

The headland overlooking the coast and the estuary of the Tyne, where Tynemouth Castle is to be found, is not actually in Northumberland. At least, not since the bureaucratic re-shuffling in 1974 created the Metropolitan Borough of North Tyneside which pushed the county boundary a few miles north to Seaton Sluice. Before that it was either Northumberland or Northumbria depending on what age of history you inhabited. The history of Tynemouth is so deeply engaged with Northumbrian Kings, religious governance and the architects of war that it would be wrong not to include it here, in spite of what the politicians of the 20th century might have thought.

Historically, there are a number of separate elements to the site at Tynemouth. It is likely that there were pre-Roman, Iron Age settlements here from about 1200 BCE, but there is little evidence of Roman occupation. This is perhaps surprising as the castle not only commands an exceptional vantage and observation position over the river estuary and the North Sea approaches, but also because Hadrian's Wall ends not far from here on the north bank of the Tyne and the Romans would have been swarming all over the place at Segedunum, just down the road at Wallsend.

What remains today are the ruins of the old Priory, the remnants of the castle, and more recent structures - World War II gun emplacements, associated military structures and modern coastguard observation and facility buildings. There is also a large cemetery and grassed areas with picnic tables, well placed for the spectacular panorama overlooking the Tyne estuary, from the north pier across the water to the south pier at South Shields and beyond into county

Durham. It's a measure of how this place held such a highly significant and important status that 3 kings were buried here - Oswin in 651, Osred II in 792 and Malcolm III King of Scotland who met his end at the Battle of Alnwick in 1093.

The histories of all these elements, but especially the Priory and the castle, are inextricably linked and it is not possible to consider any one to the exclusion of the others. Thus, the development of the Priory, its decline, reincarnations, fortifications and evolution occurred alongside the development of the castle.

The elements of the castle and priory site sit on the headland at Tynemouth, including the castle gatehouse, the priory, the cemetery and the modern structures of the 20th century world-wars and coastguard facilities

There wasn't much here when the earliest part, the Benedictine Priory, was founded back in the 7th century. Unfortunately, it didn't last long and, although fortified by the monks, within 100 years the Priory suffered attacks by the Danes who devastated much of it in 875. It was regularly attacked by the Scots too, and by the time the Normans turned up in the 11th century it had been abandoned.

The site attracted the attention of William the Conqueror's Norman invaders who began the construction of fortifications there, at that time in earth and wood. Thus the castle and the Priory site existed and developed more or less alongside each other.

There were attempts to re-found the Priory in 1090 by Robert de Mowbray, Earl of Northumberland. However, having killed Malcolm III of Scotland at Alnwick, Robert then did a political U-turn and rebelled against King William II of England. That didn't go down well with the English, so he took refuge in Tynemouth Castle. William, much miffed, besieged the castle and captured it, and although Mowbray escaped to Bamburgh he seems to have taken leave of his senses and returned to Tynemouth where he was arrested, hauled off and imprisoned for life for treason.

During the 13th century the Priory had its ups and downs, but in recognition of its strategic position a licence to crenellate[4] was granted in 1296 and the monastery was surrounded with walls of stone. It was attacked by Robert the Bruce in 1314 but successfully defended, and to add to its strength a gatehouse and barbican were added on the landward side of the castle in 1390. This is very much what can be seen today – the quite spectacular ruins of the old Priory and the castle gatehouse and walls. Although the headland was originally completely enclosed by a curtain wall and towers it was not well maintained. Eventually the north and east walls fell into the sea, and most of the south wall was demolished. The west wall, the gatehouse and a section of the south wall, with the original wall walk, remain in good condition today.

The castle has its place in the Arts as well as in history. In 1312 King Edward II took refuge in Tynemouth Castle together with his pal Piers Gaveston, before they fled by sea to Scarborough. These events were dramatised by Christopher Marlowe in his play Edward II, published in 1594. Scenes in the play are set *'Before Tynemouth Castle'*, *'Near Tynemouth Castle'* and *'In Tynemouth Castle'*. Even Marlowe recognized the status of this Geordie stronghold!

Guns both ancient and modern are displayed in recognition of the centuries of warfare in which this site engaged
Photos Ken Lussey

Inevitably, in 1538 the monastery of Tynemouth, like so many others, met its end during Henry VIII's program of dissolution. In practice this meant that the physical stonework was substantially dismantled. However, what was left of the monastery was put to military use, fortified as a supply base for the Scottish campaigns. With its now exclusively military function new and better guns were installed. In 1545 new defences, across the bay from the headland, enabled guns to fire directly on the river mouth, which they had been unable to do before. This became the Spanish Battery, allegedly named after Henry VIII's Spanish mercenaries.

In the 17th century the conflict between Crown Royalists and those who supported a Republican parliament turned into a full-on war[2]. Although Tynemouth's guns controlled the river, Newcastle and Tynemouth were forced to surrender after the Battle of Marston Moor in 1644 when Oliver Cromwell's Parliamentary forces defeated Charles I's Royalists and the Crown's cause in the north collapsed.

King Charles II was restored[11] to the throne of England in 1660, and Tynemouth continued as a military garrison. Much of it was demolished in 1665 by the then Governor, Colonel Edward Villiers who had other ideas for its use. He built a new barracks, a lighthouse and a house for himself which included servants' quarters, stables, a brewhouse, barns and stores, using stone and lead from the demolished priory buildings. In 1672, during the Anglo-Dutch Wars, a defensive gun battery known as Clifford's Fort was built on the riverside near the mouth of the Tyne. This reduced the need for the guns positioned at the castle, and by 1681 the castle had diminished in military significance and had only a "slender garrison".

Ron Lyons

There was some revival of the castle's function during British involvement in the French Revolutionary War (1793–1802) and Napoleonic Wars (1803–15), when the site was utilized as an ordnance depot to supply the troops with ammunition. New barracks were built, and gun platforms constructed on each side of the gatehouse to defend against any attack from the landward side.

At the end of the Napoleonic Wars in 1815, the ordnance depot closed but in the mid 19th century with the growth of riverside industries - shipbuilding, the export of coal and the building of Armstrong's armaments factory at Elswick - Tynemouth's defences were improved with new guns, a new gunpowder magazine, barracks and stores. By the 1880s, new piers at the mouth of the Tyne had blocked the field of fire from Clifford's Fort at river level and so Tynemouth Castle and the Spanish Battery became, once again, responsible for protecting the river and its industries from long-range fire from warships and raids by small torpedo-carrying boats.

A fire in 1936 destroyed much of the barracks and several other buildings. During World War II it was used as a coastal defence installation and suffered air raids in 1941, but after the war all military function ceased. Civil coastguard activities continued for a while and a new coastguard station was built in 1980, but that closed in 2001.

The feet of many men have stood on this headland over the centuries – men of religion, men of politics and power, men of war and men of trade. Today, the site has been stripped of its military structures and the priory and the castle remain as historic monuments for the modern visitor to explore. It is all brought together by the interactive 'Life in the Stronghold' exhibition (located in the Warrant Officer's House) which takes visitors on a journey from Tynemouth's beginnings as an Anglo-Saxon settlement, a medieval monastery and Tudor fortification, right up to its importance as a WWII coastal gun battery.

Ron Lyons

The green spaces and picnic areas amidst the old stones and towering ruins of the Priory are quiet, peaceful places. Yet, not many yards upriver from here is the industry of the Tyne. Although no longer loud with the clamour of rivet hammers and the machines of shipbuilding, there is industry nevertheless in the ferry terminals and bonded warehouses that line the river. As one regards this modern, commodity driven industry it's sobering to think that for most of the lives of both the Priory and the castle none of that existed, and that the view from the castle promontory here would have been but bare riverbanks, rolling Durham hills and the grey expanse of the North Sea.

The ruins of the old priory and castle stand as iconic features on the southernmost reaches of old Northumberland.

Stewardship/Management – English Heritage

www.english-heritage.org.uk/visit/places/tynemouth-priory-and-castle

NE30 4BZ

Guidebook – available on site or from English Heritage

Admission: Charges apply; **Parking**: Local pay and display; **Opening** Scheduled opening times; **Toilets**; **Café/Restaurant** local facilities; **Gift Shop**; **Exhibitions/Displays**; **On-site Management**; **Dogs** on leads only; **Disabilities:** Some disabled parking on site; generally accessible with some area exceptions

Resources and Further Reading

- englandsnortheast.co.uk/tynemouth/ [*a history of the area and its development*]
- www.gatehouse-gazetteer.info/English%20sites/2023.html [*extensive historical and architectural information*]

THIRTY SIX

ENGLISH HERITAGE

WARKWORTH CASTLE

Warkworth Castle is a ruined medieval fortress overlooking the village of Warkworth in the coastal region of east Northumberland. It is a Grade I listed building and a Scheduled Ancient Monument, under the management of English Heritage since 1984. From the 14th to the 17th centuries it was the favoured residence of the powerful Percy family, the Earls (and later the Dukes) of Northumberland. The Percys were among the most prominent landowners in northern England, making Warkworth a significant and prestigious seat of nobility.

Although the settlement of Warkworth dates back to at least the 8th century and the Anglo-Saxon Earls of Northumbria, the first castle was not built until after the Norman Conquest. Less than a mile from the coast and the seaside town of Amble the castle occupies a naturally defensible spur of land created by a tight loop in the River Coquet, protecting the ancient Anglo-Saxon town of Warkworth and dominating the surrounding countryside.

Warkworth castle dominates the skyline, as seen from the estuary of the river Coquet

Its construction is usually attributed tò Prince Henry of Scotland, Earl of Northumbria, in the mid-12th century, but it may have been built by King Henry II of England when he took control of England's northern counties. Either way, Warkworth Castle was first mentioned in a charter of 1157 when Henry II granted it to Roger fitz Richard, a member of a noble Norman family. However, the timber castle was considered feeble, and was left undefended when the Scots invaded in 1173.

Roger's son Robert fitz Richard inherited and improved the castle. Many features visible today date from this period, including the gatehouse - originally accessed via a drawbridge with two gates, one at either end of the passage, and a portcullis - Carrickfergus Tower, postern gate[1] and east curtain wall. Robert was quite a chum of King John, and hosted him at Warkworth Castle in 1213. Although the castle remained in the fitz Richard family line, a descendant John de Clavering, with what may be considered to have been a bit of toadying up to the King, made the Crown his inheritor. With the outbreak of the Anglo-Scottish Wars and under Crown control, Edward II invested in Warkworth, where he funded the strengthening of the garrison in 1319.

Between roughly 1310 and 1330 the English struggled to deal with Scottish raids in northern England. Twice in 1327 Scottish forces besieged the castle at Warkworth, but without success.

The great gatehouse *Fred Vincent*

John de Clavering was declared bankrupt owing large sums to an Italian merchant, and died in 1332. His widow died in 1345, at which point the fitz Richard tenure at Warkworth Castle came to an end, and the 2nd Baron Percy of Alnwick took control. Although the Percys owned Alnwick Castle, which was considered more prestigious, it seems that Warkworth was the family's preferred home. Under the Percy family a park was created nearby for hunting, and within the castle two residential blocks were created, described as "*of unparalleled quality and sophistication in Northumberland*". Henry Percy, 1st Earl of Northumberland and father of the celebrated Harry Hotspur, added the imposing keep overlooking the village in the late 14th century, which was likely to have been intended to cock a snook at John of Gaunt and his nearby Dunstanburgh Castle. The castle at Warkworth in the 14th century must have been a handsome, prestigious place.

The 1st Earl and his son Henry "*Harry Hotspur*" Percy were a rebellious pair, and played an active role in deposing Richard II in 1399. Through their various allegiances with forces against the Crown the Percys were in and out of disgrace, and the castle at Warkworth in and out of their control, forfeited to the Crown one minute, then restored to them the next, on several occasions in the early 15th century.

Ron Lyons

During the Wars of the Roses[3] the Percys supported the House of Lancaster and thus Parliament. For this unacceptable allegiance King Edward IV issued an attainder[12] against the family and their property was confiscated. The title of the Earl of Northumberland was given to the 1st Marquess of Montagu, a Yorkist, and with it, the castle. During his tenure, he constructed a twenty five feet tall rectangular tower, to this day known as *'Montagu's Tower'*.

In 1470 Edward IV returned the Percys' estates to the eldest son of the third earl, who was also called Henry Percy. The Percys seem to have suffered a spectacular lack of imagination when naming their male heirs, but anyway a year later this Henry was granted the earldom of Northumberland. Sometime after 1472 Henry remodelled the building of the bailey, and also planned to build a collegiate church within the castle, but the work on the church was abandoned after his death. When the fourth earl was murdered in 1489, his son, Henry Algernon Percy, inherited and maintained the castle. In the early 16th century another Henry, the 6th Earl of Northumberland, removed most traces of the incomplete church. Thomas Percy, brother of the sixth earl, was executed for his role in the Pilgrimage of Grace[10] in 1536, and when Henry Percy died the next year without any sons, the family's property passed to the Crown.

Fred Vincent

This might well have ended the Percys tenure at Warkworth but in 1557, by which time the castle had fallen into disrepair, the estates were restored to the descendants of Thomas, and the nephew of the sixth earl, another Thomas Percy, was given the earldom, and he began a programme of repairs.

The Catholic Thomas Percy joined the rebellion known as The Rising of the North[8] in 1569 that sought to re-establish Roman Catholicism in England, and his supporters congregated at the castle. Sir John Forster, Warden of the March, intervened with force and the castle was surrendered to his control. During the conflict that followed, Warkworth remained under royal control and Forster used the opportunity to pillage it, stripping it of timbers and furnishings, although the keep itself remained intact. In the meantime and for his misplaced allegiance an attainder[12] was issued against Thomas Percy so that when he came into English custody he was executed without trial. As a result, Thomas's son was passed over, but under the terms of the attainder his brother was allowed to inherit. In 1574, Elizabeth I granted Henry Percy (another one) permission to inherit the family's property and assume the title of 8th Earl of Northumberland.

Yet another Henry Percy inherited the family estates in 1585 and assumed the title of 9th Earl of Northumberland. However, the Percys were heavily implicated in the failed Gunpowder Plot of 1605 and the earl was imprisoned for his connection with the plotters. Shortly before he was sentenced the earl leased Warkworth Castle to Sir Ralph Gray, who owned Chillingham Castle. Gray neglected the castle and allowed it to fall further into disrepair, with lead from the buildings being sold off. When James I visited in 1617 en route to Scotland, he was angered by the sorry state of the castle, but with the unification of England and Scotland under a single ruler, the earls of Northumberland had no need for two great castles near the border. Alnwick was maintained at the expense of Warkworth.

Well-preserved interiors, including banqueting rooms, cellars and kitchens, as well as the battlements and towers can all be explored at Warkworth

Ken Lussey

The deterioration of the structure continued during the English Civil War[2]. Parliamentarian forces took over the castle in 1648 and when they withdrew they slighted[9] the castle, removing the doors and iron so that it could not be reused by the enemy.

The 11th Earl of Northumberland, the last Percy earl, died in 1670, and two years later his widow allowed the keep's materials to be reused in the building of Chirton Hall. The property then passed to The 7th Duke of Somerset through marriage, and in 1698 the owners decided not to renovate Warkworth Castle due to the expense of doing so. Lady Elizabeth Seymour inherited the property from her father in 1750. Her husband, Hugh Smithson adopted the surname "Percy", the dynasty of the Dukes of Northumberland through whom possession of the castle then descended.

During the 18th century the castle was allowed to languish. The south-west tower was falling apart and around 1752 part of the curtain wall east of the gatehouse was demolished, although later rebuilt. The 3rd Duke of Northumberland undertook some preservation work and his successor, the 4th Duke, carried out some work to restore the keep between 1853 and 1858, but the work done was limited and did not effect a full restoration.

The castle dominates the village, the loop of the river Coquet and the approach from the coast
Photo Fred Vincent

By the early 20th century the castle was obviously beyond any restoration which might allow the place to be habitable. In 1922 The 8th Duke of Northumberland granted custodianship of the castle to the Office of Works, succeeded by English Heritage in 1984. The castle continues to be officially owned by the Percy family, currently the 12th Duke of Northumberland.

One cannot consider the castle at Warkworth without at least a mention of The Hermitage, the remains of a small, primitive chapel, carved directly out of the cliff rock a few hundred yards up-river. It was probably established as a private chapel by the 1st Earl of Northumberland in about 1400, but another piece of folklore has it that it was built by a knight who tried to rescue his lover from Scottish raiders. Unfortunately, so the story goes, he accidentally killed her and his own brother. How he managed that is not recorded, but devastated by his loss, or perhaps his breathtaking incompetence, he gave away all his worldly goods and became a hermit. Set amongst the copious overgrowth of ivy and vines The Hermitage is accessible only by boat, and on the bank path a resourceful boatman awaits the presentation of your wallet in exchange for a quick row across the river and, if you're lucky, back again.

The Hermitage

Simon Hawkins

The village of Warkworth is stupendously pretty. The wide main street runs downhill from the castle hill through an eclectic mix of small shops, cafes, pubs and cottages. Northumberland stone abounds. The old medieval bridge with a fortified tower at one end, built in about 1380, spans a dark, lazy river Coquet. Walks along the river bank are easy, leafy and relaxing. All this under the watchful walls of the castle and its pennant flying from the topmost tower. And if you're taken by a fancy for some fish and chips the seaside town of Amble is but a short walk away.

Stewardship/Management – Percy family/English Heritage

www.english-heritage.org.uk/visit/places/warkworth-castle-and-hermitage

NE65 0UJ

Guidebook – available on site or from English Heritage

Admission: Charges apply; **Parking**: On site charges apply, free roadside in village; **Opening** Scheduled opening times **Toilets; Refreshments** vending machine on site, facilities in village; **Gift Shop; On-site Management; Dogs** on leads only; **Disabilities:** Good disabled access at ground level, restricted within castle

All facilities are available in the village of Warkworth only a short walk away

Resources and Further Reading

- en.wikipedia.org/wiki/Warkworth Castle [*the Wikipedia entry is particularly full and illuminating on the history of the castle*]
- Warkworth Castle and Hermitage [1990] [English Heritage] Honeyman and Blair
- Warkworth Castle (English Heritage Red Guides) [2006] John Goodall
- www.gatehouse-gazetteer.info/English%20sites/2879.html [*detailed historical and architectural information*]

GLOSSARY

[1] Postern Gate: a secondary entrance in a fortified structure, such as a city wall or a castle's curtain wall. Usually small and relatively inconspicuous, postern gates were found at the side or "*round the back*" and allowed secretive or tactical means of entrance, escape or attack.

[2] English Civil War: actually a series of civil wars from 1642 fought primarily over the balance of power between Parliament and the monarchy, essentially Charles I. In June 1646 the Royalists were defeated and the king taken into custody. Charles was executed in 1649 and the Parliamentarians held government under Oliver Cromwell until the monarchy was restored to his son, Charles II, in 1660. See [11]

[3] Wars of the Roses: (1455–1487), a series of civil wars fought over control of the English throne in the mid-to-late fifteenth century, contested between supporters of two rival branches of the royal House of Plantagenet, the Lancastrians and the Yorkists.

[4] Crenellation: a defensive architecture - the battlements, parapets and general fortifications installed on a building. Typically, embrasures in a parapet to allow for the launch of arrows or other projectiles. A licence, known as a "*licence to crenellate*" was required to add this to a building during 12th – 16th centuries.

[5] Union of Crowns: The accession of James VI of Scotland to the throne of England as James I in 1603, following the death of his cousin Elizabeth I who died without heir, thus bringing England and Scotland together under a single monarchy.

[6] Pele Tower: a small, fortified keep or tower house mainly dating from 14th – 17th centuries. Free-standing, defensive structures, they also served as watch-towers.

[7] John Dobson: a 19th-century, much celebrated, English neoclassical architect. Dobson was born in North Shields and was involved in the design of many iconic buildings in the north east, including Newcastle Central Station, Eldon Square, The Royal Arcade and many others. He was also responsible, or partly so, for the design of many of the castellate houses and manors throughout much of Northumberland.

[8] Rising of the North: also called the Revolt of the Northern Earls or Northern Rebellion, in 1569 it was an unsuccessful attempt by Catholic nobles from Northern England to depose Queen Elizabeth I of England and replace her with Mary, Queen of Scots. The rebellion was led by Charles Neville, 6th Earl of Westmorland, and Thomas Percy, 7th Earl of Northumberland.

[9] Slighted: dismantled or destroyed sufficiently to be put beyond effective military function.

[10] Pilgrimage of Grace: a popular revolt against Henry VIII's break with the Catholic church and the dissolution of the lesser monasteries. The revolt began in 1536 and spread to northern England, including Northumberland.

[11] The Restoration: the restoration of the Stuart monarchy to the throne of England in 1660 when Charles II returned to the throne after exile in Europe and following the collapse of

Parliamentary rule precipitated by the English Civil War, commonly associated with Oliver Cromwell.

[12] Attainted: the condemnation, dishonour or disgrace of someone adjudged to have acted against *[usually]* a higher authority such as a monarch. It frequently attracted a sentence of death or the confiscation of land, property and title.

[13] Solar Tower: a room in many medieval manor houses, great houses and castles, mostly on an upper storey, designed as the family's private living and sleeping quarters. Within castles they are often called the "*Lords' and Ladies' Chamber*" or the "*Great Chamber*" and a room of comfort and status. The solar tower, or room, was almost ubiquitous among late castles across the British Isles

[14] Border Reivers: robbers, plunderers and raiders along the Anglo-Scottish border from the late 13th century to the beginning of the 17th century. The reivers were both English and Scottish and raided both sides of the border impartially. Usually after horses and cattle, raiding parties armed with swords, bows and crossbows, lances and knives might range from a few dozen to organised campaigns involving up to three thousand.

Acknowledgments & Resources

Although many people have engaged with me in my research for this book, I would especially like to thank the following for their assistance, co-operation, contributions and photography:

Jonathan Elkington of **Chipchase Castle** and his professional photographer **Neil Denham.**

Francis Watson-Armstrong and his wife **Claire** of **Bamburgh Castle,** and his Collections and Conservation Manager **Lisa Waters**

Victoria Perkins, marketing manager at **Alnwick Castle**, and her colleague **Daniel Watkins**

Sir Humphry Wakefield of **Chillingham Castle** and photographer **Darren Chapman**

Simon Hawkins of **Fabulous North**: Simon's website at *https://fabulousnorth.com/* is dedicated to the fabulous places and hidden gems of Northumberland, Tyne and Wear and the North of England and includes many excellent photographs, visitor information and personal experiences.

Fred & Sue Vincent of **Castle Finders:** Fred's website at *https://castle-finders.co.uk/* is a quest for the long lost and forgotten castles, and from their ruins he resurrects their history & legends, inspiring personal adventures.

Ron Lyons of **Great Castles;** although Ron is American, from Edgewater Maryland, he brings a fascination for European history and castles in particular. With his colleagues Richard Jones and Seth Friedman their website at *https://great-castles.com/* brings a wonderful collection of history, photographs and fascinating facts.

Andrew Herrett of **CastleFacts**. Andrew's comprehensive website at *http://www.castlefacts.info/*describes itself as "*a comprehensive photographic database of the medieval fortifications of england and wales*". It's a remarkable resource and well worth exploring.

Ken & Maureen Lussey of **Undiscovered Scotland**. Ken & Maureen's website is an exceptional resource for almost everything you would want to know about Scotland and the north east of England. Not just castles but accommodation, tours, holidays, places of interest and much more. *https://www.undiscoveredscotland.co.uk/index.html*

Derek Taylor, a Morpeth man and a collaborator with me on my previous book "*Northumberland: the Coast*" Derek has a passion for Northumberland and is a photography contributor to the Campaign for the Protection of Rural England. He has graciously allowed me to feature some of his work in this book, as has **Paul Turner**.

From Facebook I acknowledge the contributions of **Keith Mitchell** who, with his colleagues, maintains the sites of **Northumbrian Coastline** and **Northumbrian Castles**, where contributors' comments and photography cannot fail to inspire their readers.

Other than the above, I would like to recommend the following resources which will offer the reader yet further opportunities to explore:

Perhaps first and foremost, the academic, researcher and author **Dr. Dan Jackson** whose book "**The Northumbrians**" is a highly acclaimed work on the history of the north east. I can do no better than to repeat the Sunday Times' glowing review – "*Superbly researched and written with immense affection, Jackson's history of northeastern England has a fascinating nugget of information on every page … [this is a] hugely impressive book*".

Otherwise, the following online resources all offer their individual takes on the castles of the north east:
visitnorthumberland.com; historic-uk.com; britishcastle.co.uk; www.castrumtocastle.com; www.famouscastles.net; www.britainexpress.com; co-curate.ncl.ac.uk; www.castleuk.net; www.discoveringbritain.org;

Finally, but not least, my editors **Doug Hermann** and **Gillian Atterson** whose expertise has ensured that my manuscript contains fewer grammatical, syntax and punctuation errors than it otherwise would have done.

Author's Note

When I was a child in the 1950s and 1960s it was common for my parents to take my brother and me for a day out, away from urban Tyneside to the countryside and the further reaches of Northumberland. The castles were a popular destination – Warkworth, Bamburgh, Alnwick and many others. Over the decades since then I've often returned and I'm able to say that I have, at one time or another, personally visited every one of the sites featured in this book, most more than once and many several times.

In the course of preparing and researching this book I have approached all of the owners or management institutions responsible for each site. Many have responded with welcome enthusiasm and provided me with valuable assistance in making sure the text is accurate both in historical and contemporary terms. In other words, I've been fact-checked by the people who actually run these places – something of a comfort when research can be littered with false trails and unreliable information.

The same owners and managers have also provided me with photographs from their own collections, many of which I would have been unable to source elsewhere, and given their permission for me to use them in this book.

ABOUT THE AUTHOR

I was born on Tyneside and spent my childhood and adolescent years there surrounded by the business of shipbuilding (my father was a naval architect) and the seaside resort of Whitley Bay. I was educated at Barnard Castle School on the Durham/Yorkshire border, and at De Montford University, Leicester where I gained an Honours degree in law. My career took me to East Anglia where I eventually became a senior partner of a Norfolk law firm.

Outside of writing, I enjoy painting, the fells of the Lake District and the wide landscape of Northumberland, exploring my heritage and reading. I enjoy many genres of writing, from Daniel Defoe to Sebastian Barry. I am especially drawn to contemporary travel writers such as Michael Palin, Paul Theroux, Pete McCarthy and Bill Bryson, but perhaps the real joy is in discovering authors new to me, both old and new.

I am also drawn to the culture of the English pub. I love the chance meetings and the unexpected encounters one can experience when just idly resting an elbow in a comfortable, well-stocked bar.

I am now retired and live in the city of Norwich with my wife and cat.

ALSO BY THE SAME AUTHOR:

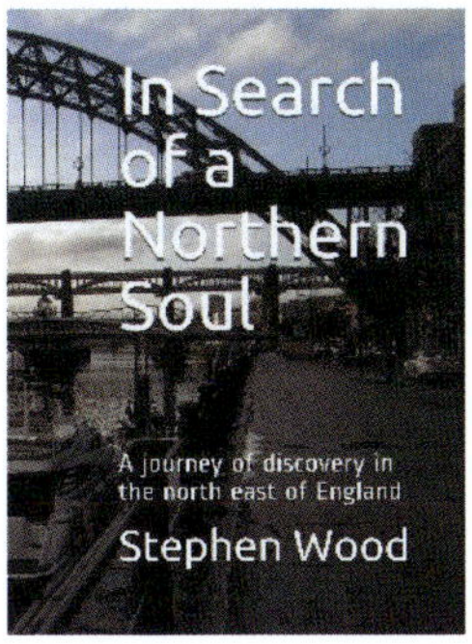

In Search of a Northern Soul – a journey of discovery in the north east of England.
(published 2020)
A deeply personal but light-hearted and humorous look at the land of the author's birth and heritage. This is an adventure into both the present and the past landscapes of the north east of England, a journey that is light, playful yet often poignant and thought-provoking, exploring the places in which his ancestors lived and worked, looking for their memories and exploring far back in the depths of his own memory for the seeds of their experiences. Not simply a travelogue but heritage, history and beer.

Northumberland: the Coast - a journey through the coastline of Northumberland, with photography by the people of Northumbria.
(published 2021)
From the Tyne and the resorts of Tynemouth and Whitley Bay, through the industry of Blyth to the wide expanse of Druridge Bay; past Amble, Alnmouth, Boulmer, Craster, Embleton, Low Newton, Beadnell, Seahouses, Bamburgh and Lindisfarne to arrive at Berwick, the northern boundary of the county and the Scottish border. Amidst the villages are scattered the bays, promontories, coves and sands of this sparsely populated landscape.
A journey that will amuse and invoke memories, curiosity and enthusiasm for this wonderful Area of Outstanding Natural Beauty.
"A wonderful record of a journey through a fabulous landscape"

Northumberland: the Coastal Pubs and Inns – encounters with the landscapes, histories and contemporary settings of Northumberland's coastal pubs & inns.
(published 2022)
Many of Northumberland's coastal pubs & inns were born from the ancient industries of the coast – fishing, exporting coal and grain, and of course smuggling – and they all have their stories to tell.
With 30 pubs, over 100 photographs and more pints than you could shake a stick at, this is a book that will engage, amuse and inspire anyone who enjoys the county of Northumberland, bar stools, and everything that makes up that worthy English institution – the pub.

Full details, blogs, contact, projects and shop at

www.stephenwoodauthor.wordpress.com

Contact
swoodnorwich@gmail.com
07990 970 980

24, Rose Valley
Norwich NR2 2PX

Orwell House

Printed in Great Britain
by Amazon

26128721R00098